MW01489616

HOW TO SELL ON EBAY FOR BEGINNERS

EBAY SELLING SECRETS FOR EASY ONLINE SALES

**MONEY MAKER
PUBLISHING**

Copyright 2022 - All rights reserved.

This document is geared towards providing exact and reliable information in regards to the topic and issue covered. The publication is sold with the idea that the publisher is not required to render accounting, officially permitted or otherwise qualified services. If advice is necessary, legal or professional, a practiced individual in the profession should be ordered.

- From a Declaration of Principles which was accepted and approved equally by a Committee of the American Bar Association and a Committee of Publishers and Associations.

In no way is it legal to reproduce, duplicate, or transmit any part of this document in either electronic means or printed format. Recording this publication is strictly prohibited, and any storage of this document is not allowed unless written permission from the publisher. All rights reserved.

The information provided herein is stated to be truthful and consistent, in that any liability, in terms of inattention or otherwise, by any usage or abuse of any policies, processes, or directions contained within is the solitary and utter responsibility of the recipient reader. Under no circumstances will any legal responsibility or blame be held against the publisher for any reparation, damages, or monetary loss due to the information herein, either directly or indirectly.

Respective authors own all copyrights not held by the publisher.

The information herein is solely offered for informational purposes and is universal. The presentation of the information is without a contract or guarantee assurance.

The trademarks used are without any consent, and the trademark publication is without permission or backing by the trademark owner. All trademarks and brands within this book are for clarifying purposes only and are owned by the owners, not affiliated with this document.

CONTENTS

INTRODUCTION

Many people underestimate the power of eBay and don't realize the income potential that lies within this fantastic marketing platform if utilized correctly.

This book contains proven steps and strategies to sell on eBay creatively so that you can make a considerable profit by selling your products on eBay.

This book will teach you how to use your ideas with the items you can regularly find at thrift stores and other sources to profit considerably. This book is not just about finding those treasures but how you can sell them and also teaches you all the basics to start your business on eBay.

You will be walked through the different steps and procedures for launching your eBay business and given great detailed ideas that you can use to make a profit. At the end of this book, you will be given tips ensuring that you can turn a profit and that you only purchase items that you will be able to resell.

Would It be nice to know that you could make an extra dollar or even more on eBay monthly? Wouldn't it be better if you could make this much money by working 10 hours a week? I have created this book specifically for anyone looking to increase their monthly income while providing a realistic step-by-step plan of action to earn more monthly dollars on eBay. Whether you have a job or not, follow the principles and strategies throughout this guide, and you will have built a profitable stream of income that can potentially pay up to more dollars, per month, on eBay.

I'm not writing this for the lazy but for those who genuinely want to better their financial situation. You are going to have fun doing this. Follow my lead, and this will work for you.

So, let's get started. We will certainly not get anywhere when it comes to eBay if we don't get a move on learning new life implementations. But before we start, we must change any lazy mentality we might unknowingly hone. By doing this, we need first to change our mindset. We must make sure that we change how we think from the inside out. If we have a job with a schedule based from nine to five, throw this old mentality out. Because when it comes to selling items and products on eBay, it takes a lot more than a regular nine-to-five type of schedule. You will be working at least 12 hours a day in the beginning, during the start-up duration. Be sure to give yourself 'me' time. Otherwise, it could be possible for you to drive yourself insane if you happen to overwork yourself. Starting any new venture will undoubtedly be timely, but when it comes to putting time in effort into something you're interested in, the task becomes less mundane. Before you begin selling on eBay, make sure being online is something you don't mind doing daily.

To thank you for your purchase, we're offering for free the guide *Highly Profitable Items to Sell on eBay* exclusively for the readers of *How to Sell on eBay for Beginners.*

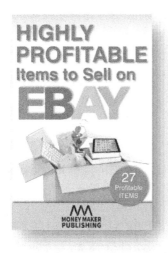

By downloading this pdf you will get a valuable list of items to sell more and more!

Click here to access your free gift or scan the QR code. Please, don't forget to leave a review if you like Money Maker Publishing! Thank you!

1. UNDERSTANDING EBAY

The concept of eBay is often misinterpreted by many people. When some look at eBay, they think of it as a place to buy cheap stuff. Others see it as an opportunity to find unique items that not everyone can access. Whatever a person's concept of eBay, one thing remains the same. People must bid for what is offered on the website.

HOW DOES EBAY WORK

As mentioned, eBay is an online auction site. Businesses and individuals can list items on the site to either sell outright or for the public to bid on. You can spend very little on an item or more reasonably priced items than you might find elsewhere. eBay makes its money by charging the sellers fees for listing and selling their items on their site.

How does this affect you? Well, you can make a lot of money from eBay in various ways. Since the fees that the site charges tend to be minimal, it makes it easier to gain a profit by selling your items with them. As you use the site more often, some promotions will limit your listing fees and make it more reasonable to list your items.

Once your item is listed on the site, the general public can view your item. If registered with the site, they can bid on your item and increase the selling price. An auction on an item typically lasts a week. At first, you might not notice much bidding going on with your item, but once the auction nears the end, it reaches the top of the list in its category and will gain more attention. Most of the bidding will take place on the last day of the listing.

After selling your item, you can track when the buyer has paid, print shipping labels, and communicate with the buyer. If the buyer does not pay for the item, you can file a dispute and get your fees refunded. After that, you can relist your item in another auction or offer it to the second-place bidder for the price they had bided for it.

eBay will charge its seller's fees once a month, and you pay by the method you choose upon opening the seller account. The fees are based upon the final selling prices of the items. They tend to be very low. However, you need to consider these fees when you are trying to calculate your profit from your item. Another factor you need to consider is the shipping and handling fees. These are typically decided upon when you list your item, but you need to know the shipping and handling prices to price this reasonably. Be careful when pricing your item for international sale because it tends to be much more expensive. I will cover more about the shipping process in a later chapter.

Understanding how the process works will help you to navigate the site better and get the most out of the experience. Getting a feel for how to sell and ensuring that your online eBay business is successful will help you sell items in the future. When you sell and raise your ratings, buyers will trust you, and you're more likely to sell what you post.

ADVANTAGES OF USING EBAY

eBay is the Big Kid on the block. They have 159 million active users with a gross merchandising volume of $100 billion in 2020. They will gladly let you tap into that market for a small piece of the action.

The best part is casual sellers can jump in and test the waters with no money upfront. Every month sellers without an eBay store can list fifty items with no insertion fees.

Name another business that lets 159 million active buyers check out your stuff? Without charging you a single penny upfront?

There are many talks out there about how you need to build your website to make it rich. The online "gurus" talk about creating niche sites. But have you ever given it a shot? It is like trying to draw your twelve-year-old away from their iPad's latest version of Call of Duty.

It is not going to happen.

What does a fisherman do when he wants to catch fish? He dangles his line where the fish are biting for other anglers.

The same thing goes when you are selling online.

You can fight your way upstream against the current. Or, you can jump right in and drop your lure where the other sellers are already hooking buyers. The choice is yours, but if you want to reel in more sales, you need to go where the buyers are. And, for the time being, that is eBay.

My thought, and what has worked best for me, is to start on eBay. Build a business that you can be proud of, then, when you are ready to spread your wings, test the waters on Amazon.

Cowen Internet Retail Tracker surveyed internet buyers in 2013. It found that 53% of respondents made purchases on Amazon and 24% on eBay. Only 11% shopped on Walmart.com, and less than 7% bought anything on Target.com.

What do you think your chances are if Walmart and Target cannot compete with eBay and Amazon?

Let me repeat it. Start with eBay. Spread out to Amazon when the time is right and enjoy the sales they will bring you.

Let's get started.

Where do you find stuff to sell?

The first question every new eBay seller asks is, "Where do I find stuff to sell?"

My answer to that question is to look around you.

It is crazy what people will spend their money on. You know the old saying, "One man's junk is another man's treasure." eBay proves that every day.

If you have not checked out what is for sale on the site, stop everything! Spend a few hours cruising through listings. Start looking at things that interest you, but do not stop there.

Browse the categories. Look at some of the stuff people are listing. It will make you think twice the next time you haul your trash out to the curb.

Let me give you a few examples:

A guy in the book category sells individual pages from a 1600s Bible. Depending on their pictures, he gets $25.00 to $75.00 per page. Dozens of people sell old magazine articles or advertisements for $10.00 to $50.00 each. Old Playboy Magazines start at $5.00. Fashion magazines with pop stars on the cover start at $25.00.

If you price it right, anything in the clothing category should find a ready buyer. Smart sellers pair pieces together into outfits. They include several pairs of slacks and blouses you can mix and match for a week's worth of outfits. I know one guy who hits the local shoe stores every week. He buys up their closeouts and resells them on eBay for two to three times he paid.

Another lady I know keeps an eye on the closeouts at Marshall's, T J Maxx, and the Gap. When the price is right, she pounces on a whole cart full of fashion essentials and triples her money selling them on eBay.

Does your town have a Big Lots? How about a Target or Walmart?

Retail stores run a constant stream of clearance sales. There is nothing wrong with the items they are closing out. Sometimes the things do not sell fast enough to justify the shelf space. Other times they are seasonal items. The store needs to change inventory at the end of the season to maximize its sales potential. That is when you need to hit their close-out bins.

Next time you are at the store, grab your cell phone. Use the eBay or Amazon app and check what some of those clearance items are selling online. It may surprise you.

Sometimes regular price items can be just the ticket you need to rev up sales.

What is your passion?

Do you collect baseball cards? Stamps? Isabel Bloom statues? Chances are you're going to find a ready market on eBay if you can offer them at an attractive price.

UNDERSTANDING EBAY CHARGES AND FEES

Yes, it is true that eBay charges for selling items on the platform. However, listing an item on eBay is generally free. You are charged when you sell the item. The amount charged by eBay for selling an item generally depends upon the price of the item, its format, listing category, listing upgrades, and the general conduct of the seller. The eBay fee charges are generally divided into two categories, i.e., the insertion fees and the final value fees.

Insertion fees

It is the fee that is charged while creating a listing prior to selling an item on eBay. Every seller is allowed 250 free listings on eBay every month, and even more if you have an eBay store. However, there are specific exclusions to these allowed free listings, which include real estate, motors categories, and business and industrial categories.

Once you have used up your 250 free listings of a month, then eBay will begin to charge an insertion fee for more listings. The insertion fee policy of eBay is as follows:

- If your item does not sell, then the insertion fee is not refundable.
- An insertion fee is charged if you list your item in more than one category.
- An insertion fee will be charged for the first listing and for relisting your item as well.

- Each listing will be charged if you create a duplicate auction-style listing for the same item.
- Your listing will be charged only once if you list multiple items with variations in one listing.

Final value fees

It is the fee charged by eBay when you sell your item. eBay charges a particular percentage of your total sales amount as final value fees as well as $0.30 on every order.

The total sales amount includes the item price, shipping and handling charges, sales tax, and any other fee applicable to your item. When you offer international shipping along with 1-day and a cheaper shipping option like domestic shipping, then eBay will calculate the total sales amount according to the cheapest shipping option offered by you. But if you don't offer any cheaper shipping option apart from 1-day or international shipping, then the total sales amount will be calculated based on the shipping service your buyer chooses. If your item is not located in the U.S. and you are in China, Hong Kong, Indonesia, Israel, Japan, Macau, Malaysia, Philippines, Singapore, Taiwan, Thailand, or Vietnam, then the total sales amount is always calculated on the basis of the shipping option chosen by the buyer.

In addition to the $0.30 charge on every order, there is an additional final value fee % set for different categories of items sold on eBay. Most of the categories charge a final value fee amount that is 12.9% of total sales up to $7500 of an item and $2.35 on the portion of the sales that exceeds

$7500. There are certain exceptions to these final value fees %, the details of which are provided on eBay's website.

An additional international fee is charged by eBay on the sales of sellers who have a registered address in the US and are delivering their items to an address outside of the U.S. This fee is also charged if the buyer's registered address is outside of the US irrespective of the delivery address of the item. The fee is calculated in the form of 1.65% of your total sales amount and is automatically deducted by eBay from your payments.

2. SETTING UP YOUR EBAY BUSINESS

Now that you have decided to launch your business on eBay, the first thing you will need to do is create an eBay seller account. Creating an eBay account is very easy and can be completed in 5 simple steps.

STEP 1

Go to www.eBay.com

At this point, you will look for the Register new account tab; it should be located towards the top of the page.

STEP 2

Register for an eBay seller account

At this stage, you will be asked to create a new user ID and password and enter a valid email and home address. In addition, you will need to verify your phone number and specify an automatic payment method for paying seller fees and for handling reimbursement charges.

Step 3

This step may not apply to everybody, but if you previously provided an anonymous email service such as Yahoo, Gmail, or Outlook account on the eBay registration page, you will be redirected to another page that requires additional information for authenticating your identity. This authentication process is pretty straightforward and will typically involve you providing a valid credit or debit card.

STEP 4

You will be asked to log into the email account you associated with your eBay account to confirm your account. This should activate your account.

STEP 5

Continue to the account settings tab and link your checking account and Visa or Mastercard debit card through which you would like to receive your eBay payouts.

HOW TO GET PAID FOR ITEMS YOU'VE SOLD ON EBAY

Sellers on eBay receive their payouts directly to their linked checking bank account. Previously, eBay used to pay sellers through PayPal accounts, but recently they have changed the process from PayPal accounts to direct bank accounts. Saving accounts are also not accepted for eBay payouts. Only checking accounts can be used for eBay payouts.

This process has made eBay payouts very simple and secure. Before you initiate a payout transaction, eBay automatically deducts its eBay fees and selling costs from your funds. eBay fees generally consist of the fees for promoted listings, final value fees, store subscription fees, and insertion fees. You can access all the information related to your eBay payments and fees in the "Payments" tab on your eBay Seller Hub.

Receiving payouts by debit card

eBay also allows you to use a Visa or Mastercard debit card for scheduled payouts, where your payouts will automatically be transferred to you on the scheduled timeline through your debit card but with a fee. eBay asks for verification of your debit card by uploading a bank statement or by use of small/ micro-charges.

If you choose the option of micro-charges, eBay will initiate two micro-charges of $1 to your card. As the micro-charges reach your bank account, you are required to sign in to your Seller hub and follow that banner instruction to confirm the micro-charges. As the verification process is successfully completed, eBay will refund the micro-charges back to your debit card.

After your debit card has been successfully added and linked to your account, there is a 48-hour security period where you are unable to receive payouts through your debit card. After these 48 hours, you can select your debit card as your preferred payment method for scheduled payouts or for on-demand payments, which are explained later in this chapter. You can then start receiving your payouts through your debit card.

However, an important thing to note here is that you will not be able to use a debit card for payouts unless you have linked a checking bank account with your eBay seller account, and at least 90 days should have passed since you registered yourself as a verified seller on eBay.

Steps of making an eBay payout

Step 1: Once your buyer has confirmed their order and paid for it, then your sales will appear as "Processing funds" in the Seller Hub. Now it is your turn to ship the order, and you don't have to wait for the funds to become available before shipping. It usually takes 1-2 days for the bank to settle eBay transactions and funds to enter the available phase from the processing phase.

Step 2: Once the funds become available, you can now wait for the payout to occur based on your selected payout schedule during account setup, I.e., weekly, biweekly, or month or you can initiate a payout on demand.

Step 3: Once a payout has been initiated, the seller hub will show you "Funds sent." Banks usually take 1-3 working days to process your payouts and make your funds available to you.

For a weekly payout schedule, the payout for the previous week is automatically initiated by eBay every Tuesday. For a biweekly payout schedule, the payout is initiated by eBay every other Tuesday, and for a monthly payout schedule, the payout is initiated by eBay on the first Tuesday of every month.

Now that you have set up your payout method, you are getting even closer to getting your very own eBay business started.

Payouts on demand

If you have already set a payout schedule to weekly, biweekly, or monthly payouts but you need an urgent payout, then eBay gives you the option of payout on demand. However, this option is unavailable for sellers who have already set their payout schedule to daily as it is their fastest option.

You can make a payout on demand by selecting the "Withdraw" option in the payments option on your seller hub or my eBay. It allows you to choose to withdraw all funds or select a particular amount. You can make payments on-demand only on available funds. Funds that are in the processing phase or on hold cannot be withdrawn on demand. Once the payout on demand is initiated, it will take about 1-3 business days for your bank to make the funds available to you in your bank account.

If you choose to use your Visa or Mastercard debit card for payout on demand, then the funds can become available to you within 30 minutes or even less, but it deducts about a 1.5% fee (minimum $0.25 and maximum $15) from the payout amount during the time of transfer to your bank account.

How can holidays affect your payouts?

It is possible that your eBay payouts may be affected and delayed by certain national or bank holidays. Daily payout schedules may be affected by one day in case of a bank holiday. On the contrary, weekly, biweekly, or monthly payout schedules can be affected by eight days, ten days, or 20 days respectively, in the case of a banking holiday.

Congratulations, you are now all set up to start selling on eBay! At this point, I am sure you are very excited to start looking for products to sell and can hardly wait to start rolling in the profits!

How to set your payout schedule on eBay?

While you are setting up your eBay account, the payout schedule is automatically set to daily by default, but you can also select between a weekly, biweekly, and monthly payout schedule.

- The daily payout schedule works from Monday to Sunday and involves all the funds that become available within the previous 24 hours.
- The weekly payout schedule works every Tuesday, and the payout of the funds that become available in the previous week are automatically initiated on Tuesday of every week.

- The biweekly payout schedule works every other Tuesday, and the payout of the funds that become available in the previous 14 days are automatically initiated on Tuesday of every other week.
- The monthly payout schedule works on the first Tuesday of every month, and the payout of the funds that become available in the previous month is automatically initiated on the first Tuesday of every month.

Here are the steps by which you can set up your payout schedule on your seller account:

Step 1: Go to the "Payments" tab on your seller hub on eBay.

Step 2: Select "Payout settings."

Step 3: Select one of the available payout options, i.e., daily, weekly, biweekly or monthly.

Step 4: Select "Save."

The payout schedule can also be changed from the "Payments" tab on my eBay.

How to track your eBay payouts?

Once a payout is initiated, eBay will send you an e-mail to let you know about it. Every payout has a unique payout ID which makes it very simple and easy to track your payouts. eBay also provides a bank reference ID for each payout which allows you to track your payout with your bank as well when needed. This bank reference ID can be viewed in the "Payout

Details" tab in your Seller Hub.

Here are the different payout statuses which may appear on tracking your payout and what they mean:

1. Created: this means that the payout process has been initiated, and a payout ID has been created.
2. In progress: this means that the payout initiated by eBay is now in the process of transferring funds to your linked checking bank account.
3. Funds sent: this means that the payout process has successfully been completed, and eBay has sent your payment to your bank account. This process could take at least 1-3 working days.
4. Returned: this means that your payout initiated by eBay encountered an issue with your bank or eBay and has been returned.
5. Blocked: this means that your payment method could be invalid, which is why your payment or payment method has been blocked by eBay.
6. Canceled: this means that some issue has occurred, which is why your payout could not be processed successfully and the payout process was canceled, and the payout funds were returned to your available funds.

What can you do if your payouts appear to fail?

If your payout status appears blocked, returned, or canceled, it is possible that the bank information provided by you is incorrect, or further information is required by eBay to initiate and complete your payment processes successfully. You can contact eBay help to further discuss the issue with them directly.

How to change your linked checking bank account to a business bank account on eBay?

If you initially registered as an individual on eBay and now wish to change to a business account, then you also need to change your linked bank account to a business bank account> Here's how you can change your account type on eBay:

Step 1: Go to the "My eBay" page and select "Account."

Step 2: Select the tab that says "Personal information."

Step 3: Select "Edit" next to account type.

Step 4: Select "Business Account" and then "Submit."

After completing this process, eBay might ask you to provide additional verification information for a business account by sending you an e-mail or displaying a banner in your Seller Hub.

What payment methods are available to your buyers on eBay?

When you create a listing for selling on eBay, the website automatically adds the available payment methods at checkout for your buyers to select from. These include:

- PayPal

- PayPal credit
- Apple pay
- Google pay
- Credit or debit card
- Spendable funds
- Payment on delivery (it should offer at least one of the approved payment methods at the time of delivery)

These are the approved payment methods that are available for all types of items being sold on your eBay store.

Apart from these payment options, eBay also provides some additional payment methods for certain categories of listings. These options include:

- Checks
- Money orders
- Bank-to-bank cash or wire transfers
- Online payment services such as Escrow, AllPay, CertaPay, Xoom, Nochex, and Fiserv.

The approved categories for the above-mentioned payment methods include coins and paper money (wholesale bullion), motors and their subcategories like boats, cars, vehicles and automotive parts, business and industry and their sub-categories like healthcare equipment, manufacturing equipment, printing, and graphic arts, restaurants and catering equipment, real estate and all the adults-only items in the everything else category.

Some payment methods that are totally unacceptable on eBay in all cases are sending cash via mail and the use of point-to-point cash transfer methods like Western Union and MoneyGram.

Once an eBay checkout is complete, you can directly contact your buyers for the selection of an alternative payment method by direct message.

What happens if a buyer hasn't paid for your order?

Once a buyer has checked out a particular order, it becomes obligatory for them to pay for their purchase within four calendar days. Suppose your buyer hasn't paid for their order within this timeframe, then you, as a seller, are allowed to cancel their order. Unpaid order cancellation is always recorded on the buyer's account, and buyers with exceptional amounts of unpaid order cancellations can face buying restrictions or even total loss of their buying privileges from eBay, but they can appeal an unpaid cancellation.

Sellers can cancel an unpaid order after four days of its placement for up to 30 days. However, if you cancel a paid order by stating the reason that the "buyer hasn't paid," then you, as a seller, can be subjected to suspension of your seller account.

TOOLS AND EQUIPMENT TO RUN YOUR BUSINESS

Now that your account is set up, you're ready to start selling on eBay! However, there are a few equipment and tools needed to run your eBay business efficiently and successfully.

Smartphone/iPhone: Be able to check items on the eBay app while sourcing for inventory to make sure you'll profit from an item. Also, have access to your linked bank account without a computer by downloading the bank app. You could also use your iPhone or smartphone to take beautiful pictures. Who needs a camera when you have the ability to take pictures with an 8MP camera!?

Shipping Supplies: Another asset to your business has shipping supplies on hand. I use the USPS flat rate shipping envelopes and boxes for shipping products on eBay. I use them because of their free! Yes, they are free, and they will even ship you out some of their shipping supplies for you free if you feel too lazy to get them yourself! How cool is that?! Did I forget that you will also need measuring tape? How else will you be able to slap on your shipping labels on your packages (unless you have adhesive labels, then you're OK)? You can get shipping tape for as low as $4 at Walmart. Who knew Walmart could be this good!

Printer and ink. You can buy a printer for as low as $50 at Walmart and ink cartridges for as low as $14 at Walmart. It's better to own your own printer to be as efficient as possible in your eBay clothing business.

That's it! Follow the steps and procedures above to setup the foundation for running a profitable business!

Purchasing the correct type of equipment for your eBay business will be an essential factor in determining the levels of success you endure.

By purchasing the correct type of equipment, you will better your chances of selling your items on eBay for top dolla become more efficient overall, and will better your money over the long haul.

Recommended equipment

- Camera or high-end cell phone
- Backdrop or lightbox
- Lighting Kit
- Laser Printer
- Computer or Laptop
- Adhesive labels
- Cardboard boxes or Free USPS boxes
- Poly Bags and Poly Mailers
- Tape
- Thank you stickers for all eBay purchases
- Cleaning products such as simple green
- Storage Boxes for inventory

Listed above are some of the essential items you will need to get you started on your path towards selling $60,000 in products your first year on eBay! Of course, this is just an essential list, and your list may include more or less depending on the type of items you sell, but for now, this should cover you pretty well.

If you decide to start selling items such as clothing, it may be wise to go above and beyond and purchase a mannequin, clothing racks, clothing hangers, a steamer, and equipment like this that tailors to your specific needs.

3. MARKET RESEARCH TIPS

T There are tons of hot products you could sell on eBay right now for profit. It's all a matter of which item you want to sell. The number of hot items on eBay that goes for killer profits is endless.

RESEARCH: MOST IMPORTANT ASPECT OF YOUR BUSINESS

Items such as clothing, electronics, games, toys, books, outdoor equipment, trading cards, and the list go on and on. Essentially, you have to find what market you want to get into. Once you've figured out which market you want to target, go even deeper to see what products are hot and what products you should stay away from. Always compare and contrast and make intelligent, calculated decisions. If I know that a Ralph Lauren Polo shirt will go for $20, then it's something to pay attention to. Why? Because you can easily source a Ralph Lauren Polo shirt for as low as $4. After all the fees have been accessed, you should have approximately made anywhere between 13-$14 pure profit.

This would be a prime example of how you would research a hot item on eBay, find it somewhere else for dirt cheap, list it on eBay, and patiently wait for that item to sell. The higher the demand for a product, of course, the faster it will sell. Ralph Lauren is a high-demand product on eBay. The good thing about selling Ralph Lauren on eBay is that the supply is HUGE, but the demand is HUGE, so they balance each other out. Typically, the genuine hot sellers are the products that are in high demand with a low supply, of course. It's all part of supply and demand, and it's no different when selling and buying on eBay.

Market research is fundamental and plays a big part in your success on eBay. Not only does market research plays a significant role on eBay, but it also dictates how much money you make. You see, market research is in direct correlation to how much knowledge you obtain in a particular market. The more you know, the better off you'll be. Never skip market research because if you do, you will never reach your optimal sales potential when selling on eBay. Market research is by far the most crucial aspect of your business, so do not neglect it. I repeat, do not neglect it. Do your due diligence and research, or get blown away by the competition. Simple.

WHAT ITEMS ARE BEST TO RESELL ON EBAY

Due to the setup of the eBay website, there are some types of items that will sell on the site better than others. Even though you will see it all when looking through the listings, some items simply do not sell and are not worth the time to buy and list. Knowing what you're looking for when doing your thrift store shopping will help you to save time and energy when shopping in a thrift store.

If you're not a frequent eBay shopper, you might not know what is getting the big bucks on it. Don't fear! We are going to explore eBay and the items you can find in your thrift store that will sell for a lot of cash. Not everything you see in a thrift store can be sold through eBay. Remember that it is an auction site, and some items do not sell well within this type of format. In this chapter, I'm going to talk about some of the items you want to consider looking for to resell on eBay that will earn top dollar. However, you might find other odd items that you can sell as well!

Electronics

Even though you might think that electronics in a thrift store might be dysfunctional and not worth the money, the truth is that some of the electronics donated can be sold for a lot of money. For example, a lot of people are looking for electronic items such as classic Sony Walkmans and other older tech items that you would initially view as having little to no value. People are constantly looking for older electronics, so just because it means little to you, it might have great value to another.

When going through the electronics section, look for items that were popular when you were a child. Old gaming systems, stereos, and other various electronics might just be a hot item for you to sell on eBay. The significant part about most thrift stores is that they provide an area to test out the item before purchase, so you can feel better about the condition of your purchase before you leave the store!

Books

Books are another item that can be sold on eBay. However, you want to find books that are either collectibles, antiques, or rare. If it's a book that can be found almost anywhere, then the buyers will pass it by. When they look for books on eBay, they are looking for books with unique characteristics, such as first editions, autographed copies, or rare books. For example, the Little Golden Books have a first edition that is worth a lot of money if found in good condition. Be aware of books and how to find the ones that can be sold in an auction setting.

Toys

Many toys that can be found in a thrift store are collectible and will sell for good money on eBay. Older toys, such as collectible board games and Barbie dolls, might be worth money if they are old enough and in demand. However, collectors won't want to buy these items unless they are in excellent or superior shape. So, before you purchase such toys, make sure that they are in decent shape or that you are able to clean them up.

Classic stuffed animals are also worth money. Get a feel for what an older toy or stuffed animal looks like and go in search of them in the toy section. Sometimes since children play with toys, you might have to dig to find what might be a great find. So, be patient and see the possibilities in what you're looking at.

Figurines and glassware

Other great items to sell on eBay are figurines. If you walk into any thrift store, you will notice that there are aisles of figurines and home décor. Take a look through the clutter on these shelves to see if you can find items worth selling. Valuable figurines will have numbers on them that will place them as part of a limited collection. The lower the number, the better chance that it will be worth the money. Also, look to see if you can find rarer forms of popular collectibles such as Precious Moments that will be worth the money.

Glassware that is older and more unique can have a significant value as well. These pieces are often mixed in with the other home décor and figurines, or you might find them in the kitchen supplies. The key to finding items that are worth money is to be patient and be willing to work through what might seem like mountains of junk.

Pens and writing accessories

It might sound silly, but people actually donate pens and writing accessories that can be worth some serious money. Thrift stores pack these in large bags and mix them with other office supplies. Many people don't know that there is value in some pens or pencils. However, pens and pencils made out of sterling silver and other metals or resin can snag some good money on eBay.

The secret to finding these is to know what types of pens are worth money and be willing to spend some time looking through all of the random grab bags to see if there is anything in them that is of worth.

Take some time and look at eBay's entire website to get an idea of what you could sell that you have seen in your thrift store. Once you see what sells, you will have an easier time finding what you're searching for when entering the doors. Knowing what to look for and where to find it is essential when finding thrift store items.

4. SOURCING

INVENTORY

When it comes to making a ton of money from your eBay business, one of the critical factors in doing so is having the ability to source profitable inventory.

While there may be a ton more ideas out there for how you can source inventory, the ideas I share with you are the ones that worked.

With that being said, try each out for yourself, see what works best, and go from there!

FINDING CHEAP ITEMS TO SELL ON EBAY

Sourcing is where you make money!

The key to finding profitable items on eBay that will let you hoard a lot of profits in your bank account is consistently visiting your sources for inventory on a daily basis. The more you go, the better the finds—always remember that! A person who sources five or six times a week is likely to find better and more profitable items than someone who goes once or twice a week. Besides, you always want to be sourcing for inventory because, ultimately, finding profitable items is what makes you money. If you are really serious about making a significant income from your eBay business, I'd recommend visiting your sources (places you shop for inventory) at least three times a week. Four times a week is preferable, but three will do just fine.

So you want to make an excellent income selling products on eBay, but you don't know where to find profitable items? Here are a few places:

- Goodwill
- Salvation Army
- Savers
- Thrift shops
- Clearance items at big-box stores
- Local dry cleaners (seriously!)
- Neighbors, family, and friends

I've found several electronics, old-school video games, golf cases, board games, books, and other miscellaneous stuff at these thrift stores, including my favorite; clothing, of course. So, get out there and go treasure hunting and have fun!

Goodwill

Goodwill stores are spread far and wide throughout the United States. Goodwill should be one of your leading go-to stores for sourcing profitable clothing items. The prices there are typically low, and you will be able to find nice clothing and other profitable items for a small investment. Look out for 50 percent off days! You should be able to sign up for your local Goodwill e-newsletter (e-mail list) and receive alerts on 50 percent off days! How awesome is that?!

Quick Tip

When sourcing for inventory at Goodwill, look everywhere! Many people tend to skip certain sections (the clothing rack on the walls, for example) because it can be difficult/tiring going through so many racks of clothing.

Salvation Army

The Salvation Army is another donation store similar to Goodwill and Savers. You can find plenty of opportunities to get great clothing and other hot items at the good old Salvation Army thrift store!

Savers

Savers isn't as popular as Goodwill, but if you have some around your area, it definitely would be wise to take advantage of the gold mine of opportunities that awaits you. Savers stores are saturated with clothes, and you may come up big.

Thrift stores

Sourcing inventory from thrift stores is a super great inventory that can make a lot of money on eBay. Having a large number of thrift stores in your area can be an excellent opportunity for you! A quick tip for getting cheap inventory at thrift stores is to go on the half-off days. Many thrift stores will dedicate a day to a special discount, or slashed rate, to keep their inventory moving. This is when you need to pounce on the opportunity and get your items dirt cheap!

Thrift shops can be an excellent source for finding inventory. When going to thrift shops, sometimes you may notice that their prices seem a little bit higher than what you're used to paying. Don't be afraid to ask for a deal; sometimes, they'll take your offer. Thrift shops are excellent sources for a wide range of inventory, especially the ones that don't know what they have!

Yard sales or tag sales

If you live in a pretty populated area, yard sales or otherwise known as tag sales on the east coast, are a terrific way to find profitable inventory for your business. I have found Saturdays to be the best day to go to yard sales in terms of finding the best inventory. Make sure if you really want to have a good experience that you plan out a route in advance the night before and you wake up early. As the saying goes, "The early bird gets the worm." This is one of the best methods for acquiring quality inventory on a budget!

Craigslist

Many people underestimate the power of craigslist and don't think that there is anything on this site besides garbage, but I am telling you right now, they are dead wrong! Craigslist is a great method to look into!

Dry cleaners

You'd assume that whatever is at the dry cleaners is nice clothing. Believe it or not, some people leave their clothing at dry cleaners, so the dry cleaners will donate them somewhere to maintain space. Instead, you can be the one they give their clothing to by offering them something in return.

Free marketing on eBay (posting your clothing pics and having a sign stating their name on eBay) would be an excellent free service to offer to the dry cleaners, and most likely, they would be happy to opt in. In short, it's a win-win situation: free marketing for your local dry cleaner and free profitable clothing for you! (This killer technique is not meant for everyone to know, so keep it a secret!)

Neighbors, family, and friends

You would be surprised at the amount of unwanted clothing (or anything else) you can get from neighbors, family, and friends. Recently, Try it out for yourself. Talk to friends, family, and neighbors about whether or not they have unwanted clothing that they'd be willing to get rid of. You just might get lucky.

5. LISTING PRODUCTS ON EBAY

W hen it comes to listing products on eBay, this is where you will make your money.

Many people struggle with listing products on eBay and tend to fail at executing this step.

The reason people find this step so tricky is because of its dry-to-the-bone nature. To be honest, there is nothing sexy about sitting down at a computer for 3-4 hours a night listing products. This task can be very repetitive, boring, and can definitely feel daunting at times!

What most people succeed at is sourcing inventory because of the adrenaline rush. There is nothing more fun than going to a thrift store on a Sunday morning searching for the next profitable item.

With that being said, we must hold ourselves accountable and commit ourselves to the list on a daily basis if we want to accomplish our goals and truly fulfill our vision.

HOW TO CREATE A LISTING ON EBAY

The topic of listing products on eBay is vast. Here are the steps required to create a listing on eBay:

Step 1: Start the listing process

Open your Seller Hub or my eBay and click the "Create listing" option in the "Listings" tab. Once you click it, you will be automatically directed to the "sell your item" form on your Seller Hub.

Step 2: Tell eBay what product you are selling

Now you have to tell eBay what product you are selling. In the search tab, write the name of your product or a product identifier and click "search." Among the search results, select an item that matches your product, and this will trigger the website to fill in your product details in the form automatically. If none of the search results match your product, then don't select any item and press "continue without selecting your product."

Alternatively, you can browse the category of your product from the "browse categories" tab. Select the relevant category or subcategory of your product.

Step 3: Enter product details

Now you will be directed to the listing form, where you need to start entering the details of your listing.

Start by uploading high-quality images of your product that clearly showcase your item with all its unique features, ways to use it, and installation if required. Images can be dragged or dropped in the browser or selected and uploaded from the browse images tab from your device or mobile phone. Images should meet the following requirements:

- They should be in either jpeg, png, gif, tiff, heic, or bmp format.
- All images need to be at least 500px on the longest side.
- If you want to upload a video of your product, then it can't be longer than 1 minute or bigger than 150MB in size.

You can also edit your photos by using the built-in photo editor of eBay. It even allows you to remove the background of your images. You can use the photo editor by selecting the pencil icon on the top left corner of each image.

Now add a title of your product which can be 80 characters long. Extra information about your product can be added in the "Subtitle" tab, but eBay charges extra fees for this.

Now select the category and store category of your item. Listing a product in more than one category requires extra fee charges.

Now you need to enter other product specifications such as brand, type, color, or other specifications which define your product and are helpful for the buyer. You can select the details from the drop-down menu or enter them manually. Add as much information as you can about your product. This enhances the customer reach of your product.

You can now add entries of the same product with variations under a single, fixed-price listing. For example, if you are selling a phone with a storage capacity of 128GB or 256GB, then you can list them both in the duplicate listing.

Now you have to describe the condition of your item under the "Item condition" tab, for example, if it is new, used, or refurbished.

Step 4: Add the product description

Now you will be provided a text field where you can enter a detailed item description that is clear and concise. It should provide all the necessary information about your item without leaving any confusion or ambiguities in the mind of the buyer. The description should be informative and not include links to any other websites.

Step 5: Enter pricing information

Now you will proceed to the "Pricing" section of the form. Here you are required to choose the listing format and set the price of your item. Add the quantity of the item available for sale. You can then choose if you want to make the product available to be bought immediately at the fixed price or if you want to set it up for auction and allow buyers to bid on your item. Here you are also required to schedule a date and time when you would like your listing to become available for buyers on eBay.

Step 6: Enter delivery details

Now you have reached the "Delivery" tab of the listing form. Here you are required to enter the shipping details and specify the terms and conditions for shipping. You will also be asked to specify the regions to which you will ship your item.

The tab will show you a "Domestic shipping" option which refers to shipping only in the U.S. If you want to ship your item internationally, select the "Add shipping service" option and choose "Additional international service" from the drop-down menu.

Step 7: Promote your listing

Suppose you want your item to stand out among other similar items and reach more buyers than you can promote your listing at this step. eBay provides several options to sellers for promoting their listings. These include Promoted Listing Standards, Promoted Listings Advanced, and Promoted Listings Express. Here you can select the type of Promoted Listing campaign for your item but note that eBay charges additional fees for promoted listings.

However, this tab also provides some free listing promotion options. This includes choosing to make the title of your listing bold so that it stands out among other similar items in search results or a Gallery Plus option where you can choose to display a larger image of your item in search results.

Here you can also provide additional offers for buyers, such as a volume pricing option. For example, you can select to provide them a particular discount on buying more than one item together.

Step 8: Set up payment and return preferences

In this step, you are required to set up the payment methods offered to your buyers for your item. Set up the return policy and specify the location of your item.

Step 9: Charity donations

Here eBay offers you to automatically donate a certain percentage of your item's price to a good cause or charity. If you want to use this option, then you just have to switch the toggle in this tab, and if you don't want to use it, then you can just skip it.

Step 10: Complete the process and list your item

Now you have reached the end of the listing process. Here the total amount of fees that will be applied by eBay to your item will be displayed. If you see the tab "List it for free," then it means no fees are applied for listing your item, but a final value fee will still be charged when you sell it.

Now click the preview button if you want to check what your listing will look like to the buyers. If you are sure and satisfied with your listing, then click "List it," and if you are unsure and need to make changes, then click "edit it again" or "save for later" if you want to list it later. This will save your listing as a draft, and you can edit and publish it whenever you want to.

And just like that, your first listing is published on eBay.

TIPS TO IMPROVE THE LISTING PROCESS

Here are ten tips for improving the process of listing products on eBay:

Create a listing routine

Having a listing routine will be crucial to your success.

Sit down right now and set a time each day you will commit yourself to listing products on eBay.

Also, write down how many items you plan on listing. Make sure you do what you set forth to do and eliminate all distractions!

Create a template for the description

A template for your description will allow you to save time in the long run. If you are selling a lot of similar items, you can create a template in word that contains product information, return policy, shipping turnaround, and anything else that would remain consistent in all your listings. Create a template, save it in word, and copy and paste it into all of your listings when listing products on eBay to save time and ensure you cover all of your bases!

Use good keywords

Using good keywords in your listing is super essential for potential customers to find your products for sale. The principal place in your listing you will want to focus your keywords are in the title. You can use a free tool called the Google keyword planner, which will allow you to discover what the best keywords are that you should use for each specific item you are selling. Check it out!

Make your best picture the main picture

You will want to make sure that the picture that best depicts your item is shown for your thumbnail. Remember, most potential customers will not click on your listing unless they are intrigued by the primary picture. Keep this in mind at all times!

Experiment with buy and now and auction formats

Depending on the items you decide to sell, you may want to focus more heavily on buy it now or auction-style listings. In order to discover which is best for your items, you will want to experiment. Take some time to do some A/B testing to see what listing format yields the best results for you.

INCLUDE MORE THAN ENOUGH INFORMATION

You need to remember that when people are shopping online, they are relying on the information you put forth in the listing. Yes, if they have a question, they can send you an email, but most won't. Give your potential customers all the necessary information they will need right then and there on the spot to make a buying decision. This alone will make a massive difference in your eBay business!

Always fill out the item specifics

The information you put into the item specifics actually has a purpose. What this section does is communicate with the eBay search engine. The more information you fill out in the item specifics, the more times your listing will pop up when customers are searching for relative information. Never skip this part!

Offer free shipping

In today's day of age, people are looking for free shipping. Now, if you are selling items that are extremely big and heavy, this may not apply to you, as it wouldn't be wise to offer free shipping, but for most items, you can build the shipping price into the list price.

Offering free shipping will not only help you to attract more customers, but it will also help you to rank higher in the eBay search engine as eBay favors sellers who offer free shipping. In addition, free shipping will help you to become a top-rated seller, which will save you money.

Offer 1-day shipping turnaround

It is a must that you offer a 1-day shipping turnaround if you want to build a profitable eBay business. Customers want their items fast and will not buy from sellers who take their sweet time shipping!

Accept returns

Returns are a must if you want to be successful on eBay. Even the big box stores like Walmart and Toys R us have to deal with returns. While it stinks to take back a return, it's just part of the business. If you fail to accept returns, you will lose out on a lot of business. Remember, most people will not return an item. For me, my return rate is typically less than 2%. Accept returns; it makes you look professional!

6. MAKING YOUR ITEMS STAND OUT

Y you're a savvy shopper, right? If you know what you're looking for, then finding it is easier if you find the items in a timely fashion. When online shopping, the products, and items listed tend to have more activity if the listing stands out in some way. Since your goal is to make money using eBay, then it's a good idea to take a look at how to make a listing stand out to the scrolling buyer. In this chapter, I'm going to give you some tips on making any item stand out in the long list of offerings that flood eBay on a typical day.

If you ever scroll through the listings on eBay, what listings stand out to you and make you want to take a closer look at them? When selling your items, you really want to make sure that your listing gets as many views as possible. Making your listing stand out is a great way to make sure that you're getting as much money from the item as possible. Let's take a look at listings that you might want to click on so that you will be able to do a similar listing for your own item.

1. Good picture

When listing your item, you want to make sure that the picture of the item is excellent and will give an accurate representation of what the item is. In order to do this, the camera needs to be able to pick up the details of the object. Try placing the item on a solid background that will complement the item and not drown it out. For items that are light in color, a darker background will help them to stand out. Darker items will stand out better on lighter backgrounds. When taking the picture, make sure that the lighting in the area is good and that the item is positioned so that it photographs well. A digital camera is excellent for this because you are able to see what you're doing and upload it to the site easily. The better your item looks on the screen, the more people will want to look at it and know more about it.

2. Descriptive title

When titling your listing, make sure that it catches your attention. A title should be descriptive and worded so that it automatically demands the viewer's attention. Look at your item and think of the different ways you can describe it, and find a catchy and unique title that will bring customers to your listing.

If it's a specific item, use the details of that item in the title. For example, you are selling a particular model of radio. Make sure that you are thoroughly describing what model it is in the title. If the buyer is not looking for that specific model, it's easy for them to pass it by without wasting time looking into the complete listing, or if they are, they know that they have found what they are looking for. However, it is crucial not to capitalize the full title of your listing. Capitalizing appears as shouting, and an entirely capitalized sentence is generally difficult to read. Instead, you can capitalize only vital terminology such as the brand name so that it stands out and catches the buyer's attention. Moreover, when reading a book, the words that stand out tend to grab your attention much more than a uniform script.

3. Low starting bid

When scrolling through the listings on eBay, I find that if the item tends to be overpriced, I will continue to search for another that is more reasonably priced. People go on eBay to find deals. Especially if you're selling used items, you don't want to price them as if they're new. If you price your item too high, to begin with, no one will want to bid on it. Try starting your item at the price you bought it for or lower and let the bidders decide the price. If it's in enough demand, the price will rise itself without much difficulty. I know that if I see items that are initially too expensive, then I will pass them by without a second glance, so don't make that mistake when listing your items. If your item is of value, you will be getting the bids that it deserves during the bidding process.

Another factor that will turn me away from an item is the shipping costs. If a seller charges more than is necessary to ship the item, then it is a massive turn-off for the buyer. Make sure that you're doing your research and placing reasonable postage on your listings. It should only cost the buyer what it would cost you to ship it.

By making your listing stand out in the auctions, you will attract viewers to look more closely at what you're selling. Once you have their attention, it is easier to have them read more about the item and ask questions about it if necessary. You want people to keep bidding on your items so that you can obtain the top selling price and gain more money from your investment. Try different methods to make your items stand out. Once your ratings start to grow, then that will become another selling point for your items. However, when you're starting out, then you will need to build your eBay business so that others will trust you.

4. Emphasize your products' positive attributes

The fact of life is that there is always something negative about everything. It might not work the way that you want it to, or it might not be the right color. However, you don't want to highlight the negatives concerning your products when selling them. Take the time and make sure you give all of the positive attributes of your products. Emphasize why it's a good product and why the buyer would benefit by having it. Be as positive as possible while being truthful.

5. Have a sufficient inventory

Before you even open your eBay shop, make sure that you have enough of your product to be able to cater to the demand. You never know, your business might be successful from the very beginning, and you will sell more than you expect. So, if you're going to offer a product, make sure that you have a sufficient inventory of it before going live with your business. It is incredibly frustrating to find something that you would like to purchase only to find out that it is unavailable!

6. Have full descriptions

Nothing can keep your product from selling more than not giving enough detail about it. People want to know as much as possible about your item. Give your buyers what they're looking for. It might seem like you're way too descriptive, but you must remember that people cannot hold and physically feel what you're selling. They want to get as much detail out of your listing as possible so that they know exactly what they are buying and whether or not they want to invest in that product.

7. Sell the features

If your product consists of many functions or parts, place emphasis on these areas when listing them. A potential buyer wants to know what the product consists of and what it can do for them. Let them know what they are getting and what it comes with. The more you can tell a customer, the more that they will consider your products.

8. Make sure you're showing what it really is

I'm sure you hate when you buy something, and it's not what you were expecting. People hate to be deceived and lied to. If you don't like it, then those you sell to won't either. Give your buyer a clear and complete picture of what you're selling and a full description that really highlights what your product really is and what it can do for the buyer.

9. Be honest

Honesty is a huge element in making sure that your products sell. As mentioned above, people hate to be lied to. They also don't want to get something that they didn't pay for. Be honest and be willing to go above and beyond for your buyers. It will help your reputation and your shop's selling abilities.

10. Show excitement in your words

If you're excited about your product, then the visitors to your shop will feel the excitement for your product. Don't let your descriptions be mundane and boring. Add life and detail to your postings. If all you're offering to the buyer is a bunch of tedious detail, they could lose interest and move on to buy a similar item from another shop. Show enthusiasm, and it will help you to sell more and draw in new customers.

11.Tell people why they need your items

Sometimes someone cannot see the need for what you're selling unless you spell it out for them. Try using this in question form. Ask them if they have experienced certain aspects that would make the product useful. For example, you're trying to sell a custom-made hat. You could use this concept like this.

> "Do you wish that your head were warmer in the wintertime? Do you want to stand out in a crowd and not have the same hat as everyone else?"

By using questions, you are getting the customer to think about their needs and wants. Play upon the fact that someone might not realize that they really need what you're selling. Also, tell them why they need your product. The hat might make them look more sophisticated. Cater to the customer's thoughts and feelings.

By making your product stand out amongst similar items, you are ensuring that the customer will pay attention to what you're selling. You might not have the products to please every person who looks at your shop, but you can at least draw attention to your shop and bring in traffic. The more traffic that you can get, the better the chances are that you're going to be able to sell something from your inventory!

7. BUILDING YOUR REPUTATION

O nce you have your business set up and ready to go, the next step to making sure that you have a successful business is to build a strong reputation that will draw people to you. The better your reputation, the more that people will seek you out and buy from you. So, how do you get a reputation that will continue to boost your business? That is something that takes time and effort, but it is possible! In this chapter, I'm going to give you a few tips on how to build an excellent reputation that will help you sell, sell, sell!

HAVE A QUALITY PRODUCT

The one thing that will get you bad reviews and a loss of business is selling something that is not of adequate quality. If you're a crafter, you want your items to be top quality. No one wants to see their creations fall apart only a few days after they make them. Ensure that what you make is top quality and will last. You don't want your customers to be stuck with something that is of poor quality. This will be the best way to make sure that your shop succeeds. If you feel that what you're selling isn't of high quality, make sure it is before you post it in your shop.

Always deliver on time

When crafting and sending your items to customers, it's essential to make sure that the product gets to your customer on time. If you're doing a customized order, make sure that you can complete it in the time promised and get it to your customer in the condition that they expect it. By delivering what you promise on time, you are one step closer to becoming much more successful within the selling world of eBay.

Customers are what make a business. In order to have a successful business, you must have customers. By making sure that your customers are happy, you are ensuring that your eBay business will be successful. Take care of your customers, and they will take care of you.

Once your buyer has made payment for the item, get the item shipped as quickly as possible. Try to ship items within twenty-four hours of purchase. The buyer likes to receive what they paid good money for quickly. If the customer has special requests about how they want the item shipped, be as accommodating as possible and follow all reasonable requests. The most outstanding amount of feedback you will receive will be centered on the quality of the item and how quickly the item arrived.

Stand by your item

If the buyer receives the item and it's not what they had expected, stand by what you sold them. If they want a refund, give them a refund upon receiving your item back. You, as a seller, want to show your buyers that you're concerned with your integrity as a seller. If you get a lot of feedback about your poor items, then you are going to have trouble selling items in the future.

Your current customers will determine how you get your future customers. Seller ratings are fundamental to making sure you sell items in the future. People look at these ratings when they look at the item. If you have poor seller ratings, it will deter buyers from wanting to bid on your item. The fewer bids you receive, the less of a profit you will obtain for the item. You want to get the maximum value out of the items you list. That's the point of trying to sell them. Take care of your customers, and they will take care of you!

Proper packaging

No one wants to have their item come in the mail damaged. This can be avoided by making sure you pack and ship the item correctly. Take some time to use bubble wrap and packing peanuts to ensure that the item will arrive in the same condition you shipped it in.

Think about it this way: the mail people don't know what is in that box. It might get thrown about, crushed, and any number of mishaps can happen during the time it leaves your hands and arrives at its destination. Plan for this when you're packing it. If it's breakable or can be damaged during shipping, take the extra effort and put extra padding around it.

Putting enough postage on it

If you're shipping without a flat rate box, then it's vital that there is enough postage on the package. For example, if what you're sending is in an envelope, then either have the post office clerk apply postage or make sure there is enough on the package yourself to ensure that it's delivered properly. The last thing that you want is to have it returned for improper postage and have to explain to your buyer that it will be longer than expected.

Insure the item

If the item is breakable and holds value, it's a great idea to purchase insurance for the item in case it's lost or damaged during shipping. When using a flat rate box, insurance is included up to a particular value. If the item's selling price is above that, make a little extra effort and purchase additional insurance on it. If the item ends up lost or stolen, at least you and your buyer will be refunded the value of the item.

Take care of your buyer. When shipping your items, treat them like they are of extreme importance. You don't know what will happen between you shipping it and the buyer receiving it. It's better to plan for the worse than under plan and have something happen. The buyer ultimately makes your ratings, so be conscientious of the different factors that can take place during the entire transaction. The buyer will be grateful, and so will you.

HOW TO AMAZE YOUR BUYER

When it comes down to it, the buyer is the most crucial part of the equation. The buyer is the one who chooses what to buy and how much they want to pay for it. In order to run a successful eBay business, you need to take care of your buyers and impress them.

The customer knows when they are a priority. Especially if you're selling a handcrafted item, you want to have an element of trust with your customers. This involves excellent communication, openness, and honesty. If you are on good terms with your customers, you can guarantee good reviews and repeat sales. In the land of business, one nasty comment will go ten times further than a positive one. So, try to avoid getting negative feedback.

If your customer wants to return your product, let them. If they feel like it's not for them, then respect that. Having a level of commitment and trust with your customers is essential for building a successful business.

Another way that I take care of my customers is by adding a personal touch to my shipments. I will add a personalized note with the product. People see this and know that I value them as a person enough to take the time to send them a greeting. Take care of your customers, and they will take care of you.

Great communication

From the very beginning, be upfront and honest about what you're selling. The worst mistake you can make is by being dishonest in how you market your item. If what you're selling has damage or imperfections, be honest about it. A buyer who receives an item that is misrepresented is more likely to give you poor ratings, affecting your future selling abilities.

If you receive questions about your items, respond in a timely manner and be honest in your communications. If the buyer is showing interest in what you're selling, give them the information that they seek. In the end, you might get a much better price for your item if you make an effort to answer all of the questions completely.

Keep your promises

Words can go a long way. There are some retailers who will say anything in order to get their products out the door. It's a matter of making money for them. If you really want to have a successful business, you won't be like that. You stay true to your integrity and your word. If you tell someone that you will do something, then do it. Telling someone one thing and doing another is a sure-fire way to make sure that your business will fail. Remember, your customers review you on this website. If you don't do what you say you're going to do, the whole eBay community will know about it. So, make it simple for yourself and keep your word. If you promise something, do it. This is the best way to build trust and a lasting relationship with the eBay community.

Give what is expected, plus some

When you describe something in your shop, then your customer is going to expect it to be that way. If you tell your customer that it will arrive at a particular time, in a certain condition, then make sure that it does it. Accidents do happen, especially when you're dealing with shipping items. However, you need to do your part to make sure that the product arrives in the condition that you promised it in.

Not only do you want to give what is expected, but go one step further and give more to your customer. Maybe the product will be in even better condition than expected, or you will add a bonus product with it. Surprise your customer with your integrity and your willingness to go above and beyond.

Pay for a tracking number

Customers like to be able to know where their items are in the shipping process. Providing a tracking number when you mark that the item has shipped will let them know where it is entire time it's in between. If something should go wrong, then the customer and you can figure out where it happened and where the package is sitting.

8. EBAY'S ADVERTISING

HOW TO CREATE AN EFFECTIVE CAMPAIGN

While eBay is the largest marketplace and comes with a built-in customer base, that also draws in a lot of competition. Having a few promotional tricks up your sleeve will help people discover your store that may otherwise not run into it organically on eBay. We've talked about a few things regarding promotion, but there are some considerations that we haven't addressed fully. The knowledge you've learned thus far, alongside this list, should make it easy for you to piece together a marketing plan that works for the amount of time and money you can spare.

Seize every opportunity

Short of being incredibly tacky, if there is an opportunity to mention your eBay store, then take the time to mention it. Telling people is the cheapest, easiest way you can possibly promote yourself. A great example of this is adding a signature to your emails that links to your eBay account.

Include advertisement in packaging

When you ship an item, be sure to include some type of promotional material. Whether it's just a thank you card with your logo or it's a full-fledged flyer with several of your commonly sold items on it. Including some type of advertisement in your packages is a very inexpensive and straightforward way to remind the buyer about the seller who just gave them a reasonable price, shipped quickly, and packaged their products safely.

Cross-promote listings

At the end of your listings, you can either link to similar listings or remind buyers to take a moment to either see your other items for sale or visit your storefront. This is a great way to lure people into shopping from you alone. If you offer video games, there's a pretty good chance the person looking at one of your games may not buy it but would buy something else of yours after realizing you have fair pricing and an excellent reputation on eBay.

Share listings elsewhere

This applies mainly to items that are either priced exceptionally well or are harder to come by. Rare items are great for sharing in other locations because people don't care if it's spam. If this incredibly difficult-to-find Bugs Bunny eraser is FINALLY on sale after not being on the market for years, some collectors are happy to hear through their usual forums and

Facebook groups that you're going to be auctioning one-off.

If you have a blog or a website, any pages that are relevant to link to one of your listings probably should link to one of your listings. If you create a high-quality blog with excellent content, the traffic generated from the blog can actually boost your business as well.

Use multiple categories

Some listings will allow you to choose two categories. While there may sometimes be fees involved, having your product in multiple categories makes it significantly more likely that potential buyers will land on your listing page and make a purchase.

Email lists

Within your package adverts, website or blog, social media, and emails, you can ask your customers to join your mailing list. A mailing list is a powerful tool for staying connected with customers that are interested in the types of products you sell or the niche these products belong to. By having a mailing list that offers its own value, you can more easily encourage people to buy products from your eBay store as well. This works best for sellers within a specific niche rather than those that sell every product they can find.

Buzz words for titles

This applies both to listing titles and the name of your eBay store should you open one. eBay specifically suggests using these words because people often use them when searching. The list includes:

- New
- Unusual
- One-of-a-kind
- Estate sale
- Specialty
- Designer
- Unique
- Rare
- Powerful
- Vintage
- Collector's Item
- Inherited

Make sure the word actually applies to your listing. While having these buzz words may help with sales a bit, being dishonest is never the correct method.

Attach a domain name to your eBay store

For those that have chosen the path of opening an actual eBay store and not just selling through listings alone, then it is wise to spend the $15 or so dollars per year for a domain name. If you run High Top Harry's Rare Rocks and Crystals, you might buy an address like "hightopcrystals.com" and simply have this redirected to your eBay store. This helps simplify the process of promotion, and it makes you look more professional as well.

There are quite a few places you can purchase a domain name.

http://godaddy.com

http://google.com/domains

http://namecheap.com

Craigslist and buy-sell-trade groups

It may seem a bit tacky to some people, but posting your eBay listings through Craigslist may not be a flawed method of pushing a few more people towards it. The same can be said about Buy Sell Trade groups on Facebook, but take the time to make sure they allow this in their group, or you may just get banned. If people try to give you grief on Facebook for spamming, don't engage them. Getting a group of people that regularly buy online angry can lead to bad feedback from bored trolls.

High-profile actions

This method isn't easy, but if you happen to find some Holy Grail type of item, it is possible to sell it on eBay, garner a ton of attention, and get a little bit of added business from it as well. Of course, you'll probably make a small fortune on this item too. There are many examples, one of the notable ones being the Nintendo Entertainment System game called "Stadium Events." There were only about 200 of these made in the United States, and this rarity and the rising interest in "retro" video games means that it has fetched as much as $35,000! Each time one appears on eBay, video game enthusiasts write hundreds of posts on their blogs, social media, and other outlets. This type of attention is great for an eBay seller, especially if it is leveraged to encourage people to check out your other, more reasonably-priced items.

9. SETTING UP EBAY SHIPPING

In this chapter, I walk you step-by-step through the process of filling out the shipping settings in your eBay listings!

For new eBay sellers, the shipping section in the listing process is by far the most confusing. However, it is actually effortless once you understand how to set it up. Trust me when I tell you that after you've done a few listings, the shipping section will become one of the most accessible parts to fill out!

You can experiment with free shipping once you are more comfortable selling, as you'll have a better understanding of your exact shipping costs, which will make it easier for you to build postage into your item cost. After all, there is no such thing as "free shipping"; someone, either you or your customer, has to pay it.

5 FACTORS TO CONSIDER BEFORE YOU SHIP AN ITEM

Before starting to set up the shipping, there are a few things you need to consider:

1. The weight of the item

The weight of the item you are going to be shipping will play a huge role in determining how to ship it most efficiently. Typically, the heavier the shipment, the more expensive it will be to ship. With that in mind, you should choose a shipment method carefully before you list an item, or your shipping costs could end up being higher than you initially thought they would be. Coming up, I will teach you about a method that will keep your shipping costs way down regardless of the weight!

2. Location of shipment

Generally, the farther away an item needs to be shipped, the more expensive it will be to ship it. If you live on the West Coast or the East Coast, you need to pay particular attention when shipping to the opposite side of the country—the price can add up quickly regardless of the weight. If this is the case for you, don't worry. I've got some tips that will keep your shipping costs down and allow you to stay profitable when on eBay!

3. Size of the item

The size of an item you are shipping can play a crucial role in determining how you are going to ship the item. Some items will have to go into a specific box because of the size.

4. Price point (how expensive the item is)

The reason you need to consider the price is that certain shipping methods are riskier than others. What I mean by risky is that depending on how you choose to ship your item, you may have a greater chance of encountering problems. For example, I have found that packages shipped standard post (the USPS method that used to be called parcel post) tend to get mistreated and broken more often than those shipped priority mail. The reason I believe this happens is that standard post, as a less expensive alternative, takes longer to arrive at its destination and therefore passes through more hands along the way. With priority shipping, packages tend to be treated more carefully due to the premium paid, and ultimately fewer hands are touching the package on its way to the destination, which decreases the risk of a problem. If you are shipping a valuable item that sold for a lot of money, it may be wise to pay a little extra to assure the item is handled with respect while in transit and arrives to your customer intact and in good condition.

5. International

When you ship internationally, you will still consider the factors you consider while shipping domestically, such as weight, location, size, and price point. However, you need to be especially careful because postage rates are so high for international shipments, and you can get burned quickly. In addition, a few things are different when it comes to international versus domestic shipping. In the next section, I will touch on those differences and a few other concerns of which you should be aware when shipping internationally.

SHIPPING SUPPLIES

Having the right shipping supplies on hand makes processing orders quick and easy!

Before you can actually list an item on eBay or ship it out, you need to have the proper supplies on hand. I am covering this topic first because I feel it is the most critical step you need to take to ensure you are shipping your packages correctly and for the best possible rate. Too often, new eBay sellers focus only on the items they are going to sell and forget all of the products needed to SHIP their orders. As a full-time eBay seller, my shipping supplies take up almost as much room as my inventory! But if you are just starting out, focus on the supplies you NEED and add to that list as you grow your business.

Computer, internet & printer

If you are going to sell on eBay, you obviously need a computer with an internet connection. And if you are going to ship from home, you also need a printer.

If you are just starting to sell on eBay and already have a printer, use it until you see a need to upgrade to a better model. Inkjet printers use a lot of expensive ink, and you have to change the cartridges frequently. If you are going to be shipping out several packages each day, you'll eventually want to upgrade your printer.

As your eBay sales increase, you may look into a printer that prints shipping labels (the kind with the peel-off backs that you can just stick onto a package) or even a thermal printer. Many online sellers these days use DYMO printers to print their shipping labels.

Digital scale

The number one supply you MUST have if you are going to sell on eBay is a digital scale to weigh packages. You can buy digital scales for around $20 on eBay, and they are also sold at office supply stores. Look for a "postage" specific scale that measures pounds AND ounces, as you'll need to know ounces when shipping via First Class mail.

You don't need a fancy model, just a tabletop digital scale that weighs ounces and pounds. If you aren't willing to purchase a digital scale for your eBay shipping, then you should stop reading this book and resign yourself to hauling all of your packages to the Post Office!

Some sellers choose to charge a flat rate for all of their orders. These sellers tend to sell the same types of items, such as postcards or clothing. For example, many clothing sellers charge $5.99 to ship clothing that weighs under one pound and ships via First Class. This results in a $1 to $3 overage depending on the weight of the package.

It's normal to pay the shipping cost a bit to cover fees, but if you choose to charge a flat rate, be careful not to overcharge. Buyers come to eBay for deals, and the shipping charges factor into that. Savvy shoppers will know you are overcharging them on lightweight items. I'll be going over weighing packages in-depth later on in this book.

If you sell a wide variety of items in various sizes and weighs, you may consider offering Calculated Shipping. Calculated Shipping charges are based on the weight of the package and the zip code to which it is shipping. Having a digital postal scale enables you to weigh these items prior to listing them so that you can enter the correct weight. Most sellers who lose money on shipping do so because they don't weigh more oversized items, causing them to undercharge customers.

However, if you have a digital scale and offer Calculated Shipping, the buyer pays the actual shipping cost based on the weight of the package and the zip code it is going to. If you have a digital scale on hand, using Calculated Shipping is a breeze. I will talk more about Calculated Shipping later on in this book.

Instead of guessing the postage costs, undercharging or overcharging, or running back and forth to the Post Office, you can save time and money by quickly printing your shipping labels from home, and a digital scale makes that possible!

Boxes & Envelopes

You can't just stick a label directly on a book and send it in the mail. Sadly, some new sellers do such things, believe it or not! Shipping packages require shipping supplies, and that means shipping boxes and envelopes, such as:

- Plain cardboard shipping boxes in various sizes
- USPS Priority shipping boxes

- USPS Flat Rate Priority shipping boxes
- USPS Regional Rate shipping boxes
- Poly envelopes in several sizes (these are perfect for shipping clothing)
- Bubble mailers in several sizes (for shipping items that need a bit more protection than a plain poly envelope offers)
- Cardboard envelope mailers (to protect items from being bent)

The great thing about the United States Postal Service (USPS) is that they offer FREE Priority Mail shipping boxes. While Priority Mail is an excellent option for shipping a lot of packages, you will need other forms of packaging for Media Mail, First Class Mail, and Parcel Select, as well as for international shipments (again, more on these forms of shipping coming up). Basically, you need two forms of shipping boxes/envelopes: Priority Mail boxes and envelopes, and plain boxes and envelopes for the rest.

Before you run out and buy new shipping boxes and envelopes, check around your house to see what you have on hand. Plain cardboard boxes, manila envelopes, and bubble mailers can all be used for non-priority mail. If you already have items on hand that you will be listed on eBay, look them over to determine the packaging you need. Perhaps you are only going to sell books, for which bubble mailers and sturdy boxes are enough. However, if you only plan to sell large items, you don't need to worry about stocking up on envelopes.

Also, avoid wrapping your boxes in brown paper. Not only is it a waste of time and money, the Post Office actually prefers that you do NOT wrap your boxes as the paper can become lodged in the sorting machines.

Packing Materials: You can't just throw an item into a box and ship it as is. You need to WRAP up your items to protect the inside of the box; I keep the following packing materials on hand at all times:

- Recycled packing paper
- Clean newspaper
- Bubble wrap
- Packing peanuts
- Tissue paper

Do NOT wrap your item in the newspaper directly; you don't want any newspaper ink to bleed onto your products. Also, make sure any newspaper you do use is clean.

In addition to packing paper, Bubble wrap is a MUST for protecting ceramics such as coffee mugs. Again, after the item is wrapped securely in bubble wrap, use newspaper to further buffer it inside of the box. If it's a breakable item, also go a step further and surround the piece with cardboard wrap OVER the bubble wrap; this creates a "box in a box" effect that further protects the item.

Packing peanuts are always lovely to have on hand to use in shipments, but buying them new is expensive. Most people are happy to get rid of the packing peanuts they have as they are a static mess to deal with. A sizeable slotted scoop makes transferring the peanuts from the container to the shipping box quick and easy.

Another shipping supply staple keeps on hand is tissue paper. eBay sells its own branded tissue paper.

Tissue paper is essential for cushioning small, fragile items such as porcelain figurines and jewelry. Since it's much thinner than newspaper or packing paper, it tucks nicely into small curves to protect delicate pieces during shipment. Tissue paper is also lovely for wrapping up clothing.

Packing Tape

So, you now have boxes, envelopes, packing paper, newspaper, bubble wrap, and maybe even some packing peanuts and tissue paper. In order to close up your packages, you need packing tape. Clear packing tape can be found at drugstores, big-box retailers, office supply stores, warehouse clubs, and even dollar stores. Packing tape is for moving boxes and isn't as strong, while shipping tape is meant to hold packages together as they travel to their destination by vehicle, boat, and/or air.

If you are just starting out, I recommend you buy a kit with the tape dispenser and some extra tape rolls. You can usually find such a kit for $10-15 in the tape section. You only need to buy the dispenser once and then tape refills as needed. Periodically throughout the year, the shipping tape at Sam's Club goes on sale.

eBay also sells branded shipping tape. If you have an eBay store subscription, you may want to use your quarterly shipping supplies coupon towards some of this tape. Not only is it great for sealing up packages, but it also acts as a sticker when you need to cover up writing that may be on repurposed shipping boxes.

Enclosures

Include a packing slip, and a business card size thank you card. Not all eBay sellers agree. However, some don't put anything into their shipments. So, whether or not to include enclosures is a decision you'll have to make for yourself. If you sell similar items, such as certain collectibles or brands of clothing, you may find it advantageous to encourage repeat buyers, and enclosures can help you do that. However, if you just sell a wide variety of random stuff, you may not be as concerned with leaving your customers with any impression of your store.

If you do decide to include packing slips in your orders, eBay makes it super easy to do, as after you print a label, there is a link you can click on to print a packing slip. The packing slip is just a copy of the original invoice that was sent to the customer when they purchased the item.

If you are just starting out selling on eBay, I recommend that you include a packing slip and perhaps write "Thank You!" on it to give it a personal touch. If you decide that you want to make eBay a real part-time or even a full-time business, you can then look into having enclosure cards printed up. The choice, however, is totally up to you!

Shipping station

Now that you have all of your shipping supplies, you need a place to prepare your shipments. If you have space, it's nice to designate an area for shipping.

Your shipping area is just as important as your inventory space, so take the time to set it up properly. A well-organized shipping station will save you time and money in the long run!

SET UP YOUR SHIPPING

Now that you know all the factors to be kept in mind, you are ready to create a listing using Calculated Shipping. It's so easy to do; here's how:

Weigh your Item

First, put your item into the box or envelope similar to the one it will actually ship out in. Note that the box doesn't have to be the exact one you will end up shipping the item in; you just want a box close to the size and weight of the one you will be using. Boxes can quickly add up to one pound of weight to a shipment, so you definitely need to get an idea of what box you will be using. While poly mailers and bubble envelopes may seem light, even they can add an ounce or two to the overall weight of the shipment.

When you are dealing with weights above 16 ounces (remember, 16 ounces or less can go via First Class Mail; and since the mug is not a book, it can't go via Media Mail), you do NOT need to know the EXACT weight; you only need to know the RANGE between pounds. Understanding that you only need to know the RANGE will make your shipping process go much more smoothly.

See how easy it actually is when you only need to know the weight RANGE? 1-2 pounds, 2-3 pounds, 3-4 pounds, etc. When an item is being shipped via Parcel Select, Priority Mail, or Media Mail, you only need to know the range of weight. There is no need to worry about being exact down to the ounce.

I mentally add 3 ounces to all packages to account for packing materials. Yes, packing paper, newspaper, bubble wrap, packing peanuts, enclosures, and tape will all add additional weight to the shipment. So, for the mug in the box that weighs in at 1 pound 8 ounces, I mentally note the weight as being 1 pound 11 ounces. However, I still don't need to put in that exact weight. I only need to put in that it is 1-2 pounds.

Mentally adding in the packaging material weight is necessary when packages are close to going to the next pound. For instance, say you have an item in its shipping box with a beginning weight (before packing materials) of 1 pound 15 ounces. Obviously, when you add in packing materials, the weight is going to bump up to over 2 pounds and will need to be listed in the 2-3-pound range on eBay. The same is true if the initial weight is, say, 2 pounds 13 ounces. When you add in another 3 ounces for packing materials, the weight will be at 3 pounds and will need to be listed in the 3-4-pound range.

Now, what about for items weighing LESS than one pound? Packages that weigh 16 ounces or less can ship via First Class. Let's say I'm listing a Christmas ornament. The ornament is small, lightweight, and fits into a

5x5x5-inch cardboard shipping box.

When shipping First Class through eBay, the weights are calculated in ranges: 1-4 ounces, 5-8 ounces, 9-12 ounces, and 13-16 ounces. My ornament falls in the 5-8-ounce range. If I list it using EBay's Calculated Shipping, I will enter 8 ounces as the package weight. Even though it is actually only 6 ounces, it doesn't matter since it falls in the 5-8-ounce range. The buyer would pay the 8-ounce rate to their zip code, and the label that prints would cover the package whether it weighs 5, 6, 7, or 8 ounces.

Free Shipping?

Many eBay sellers do one of two things when it comes to listing items at the First-Class rate: they either offer "free shipping" and pad the item's price to cover shipping, or they set a flat rate for the buyer. Let's take that ornament as an example. If I wanted to offer customers "free shipping," I would pad the selling price of the ornament by $4 to cover shipping. If the ornament is valued at $10, I will list it for $14 with "free shipping" so that I'd make my profit AND cover postage.

However, let's say I decided to have the buyer pay a flat rate for shipping. I would list the item for $10 and put in a flat rate of $4 to ship the ornament via First Class. I would pay around $3.50 for postage, and I'd apply the overage towards shipping supplies.

There are some definite advantages to offering "free shipping" on eBay. First, eBay pushes listings with "free shipping" higher in search, meaning buyers will likely see items that ship for free over those that have postage charges. Second, buyers love free shipping; even though most customers, deep down, do realize that the price of the item itself is inflated to cover shipping, many buyers prefer that the shipping is included. Third, as a seller, you don't have to worry about charging the customer the exact shipping charge on each order; even though you will have actually to pay for the postage when you print the label, it does take the stress out of making sure you aren't undercharging or overcharging on every single item.

And finally, free shipping makes it easy for customers to purchase multiple items from you in a single transaction. If you charge shipping, you'll likely get messages from buyers wanting to know how much to combine shipping and complaints if shipping is too high. However, offering free shipping may encourage a buyer to add another item or two from your store to their shopping cart.

Fill in the shipping details

So, now that you understand the shipping options and weights, let's set up the Shipping Details in an eBay listing:

After you've filled out the top half of your eBay listing, you'll find Shipping Details to be located about three-quarters of the way down the page. You will be selecting the shipping terms and services first and adding the weight last.

The first section is for Domestic Shipping. The drop-down menu lets you choose from four options:

- Flat: exact cost to all buyers
- Calculated: Cost varies by buyer location
- Freight: large items over 150 lbs.
- No shipping: Local pickup only

You can ignore the last two options; instead, you'll need to select either Flat: exact cost to all buyers OR Calculated: Cost varies by buyer location options before moving on to the next step.

Once you have chosen either Flat or Calculated, you will need to select Services. This is where your digital scale comes into play. If you have a lightweight item weighing under one pound (don't forget to add in the 3 ounces for packing material), then you will be able to choose "USPS First Class Package (2 to 5 business days)". However, you can also add in other options under that. I usually offer "USPS Priority Mail (1 to 3 business days)" for the second option. If you want to offer more than one shipping option, simply click on "Offer additional service."

As you will see when you look at all of the shipping options, there are a lot to choose from. I know that looking at all of the choices is very overwhelming for new sellers; but just remember to focus on the four I've talked about, which on eBay are listed as:

- USPS Media Mail (2-8 business days)
- USPS First Class Package (2 to 5 business days)
- USPS Parcel Select (2 to 9 business days)

- USPS Priority Mail (1 to 3 business days)

While you may select other options such as Flat Rate or Regional when you actually go to print a label, you only need to offer your buyers any one of those options in the actual eBay listing.

Handling time and cost

The next choice you need to make is your Handling time, which is the number of days it will take you to ship the item after receiving cleared payment. As eBay points out, buyers like to get their items fast, so you'll want to choose a handling time between 1 and 3 days. I always encourage sellers to ship orders out as quickly as possible.

Even though I work from home and utilize Carrier Pickup, I offer a handling time of "2 business days" offering a two-day handling time gives some wiggle room just in case you were not able to get your shipping out. However, eBay allows you to offer anywhere from same-day to 30-day handling on your items (up to 30 days is for sellers who leave their stores while on vacation). A maximum of three handling days is what most sellers offer.

The following section is Handling cost calculated shipping only. eBay is a highly competitive marketplace with millions of people buying and selling. You need to make your prices as attractive as possible, and a handling fee will only make your items more expensive.

Shipping discount

The following section is Combined shipping discounts. If you have a lot of items to sell and think that people will be buying multiples from you, you can select the "Combined Shipping Discounts" option and set up "Combined payments," "Flat shipping rule," and "Calculated shipping rule":

- The Combined payments option allows buyers to send you one payment for multiple items purchased. If you have hundreds of CDs listed, for instance, a buyer who purchases three would be able to pay for all of them in one transaction.
- The Flat shipping rule allows customers to pay the shipping on the first item and then pay a flat fee for each additional item. So, if they buy three CDs, they would pay the total shipping on one and an additional amount set by you (say, $1) for each of the other two.
- The Calculated shipping rule allows you to specify whether you want multiple items combined into a total weight for shipping or if you want to give a discount based on the combined weight.

Again, if you sell a lot of similar items, such as postcards or jeans, where you generally pay the same postage on each, either offering "free shipping" and padding the price of the item OR setting an overall flat shipping rate can work in your favor, especially if you set up a discount for customers who buy multiple items. For instance, maybe you charge shipping but offer FREE shipping when someone spends $50 or if they buy two or more items.

Note that under the "Selling Details" section above the "Shipping Details" is the option to "Require immediate payment when buyer uses Buy It Now" option. If you sell a wide variety of items and rarely sell more than one item to a customer, this is an excellent option as it will prevent people from putting the item in their shopping cart but then not paying for it. If they want it, they have to buy it immediately, not wait to pay. You can also, under the "Combined payments" section, select the "Buyers can send one combined payment for all items purchased from me within 14 days" option. Note that the immediate payment required option only works on Fixed Price listings, not Auctions.

International shipping

I honestly recommend just going with EBay's Global Shipping Program, which means you will simply ship any sold items to EBay's shipping center. From there, they will take care of all customs forms and assume responsibility for shipping the package internationally.

If you decide to opt into Global Shipping, customers will pay the postage cost to have you ship the item to eBay AND the cost to have eBay ship the item to them. Yes, customers are paying two postage costs to have their items shipped through EBay's Global Shipping. If you choose only to offer international customers the Global Shipping option, you simply check the box and move on.

However, you can opt to let buyers choose for you to ship to them directly. There are two shipping options you will use for international orders: "USPS First Class Mail Intl / First Class Package Intl Service" and

"USPS Priority Mail International." There are several other options, but if you are selling small to midsize items, these are the only two options you need to worry about:

- First Class Mail Intl/First Class Package Intl Service is for packages weighing less than 4 pounds
- Priority Mail International is for packages weighing 4 pounds for more

The weights you enter into the "Package weight & dimensions" section carry over to the international shipping options. If the item weighs less than four pounds, you can offer to ship it via First Class International; if it is over four pounds, it will have to ship via Priority Mail International.

- First Class packages must be in plain boxes or envelopes
- Priority packages can be in plain boxes or envelopes, or you can use the Priority Mailboxes

You can also use the Flat Rate boxes to ship internationally, although the Flat Rate prices are much higher for international shipments than for those in the US.

Note that you can still offer to ship orders to customers directly even if you've opted into Global Shipping. This can be an attractive offer for savvy customers who know they'll save on the shipping cost by surpassing Global Shipping. However, it does come with a risk, especially for new sellers. I personally advocate sticking with only Global Shipping until you are entirely comfortable in your eBay business.

If you do want to ship on your own outside of the Global Shipping Program, you simply click on the drop-down menu under "Other shipping options." It defaults to "None"; leave it that way if you ONLY want to ship via Global Shipping. However, you can choose "Flat: same cost to all buyers" or "Calculated: Cost varies by buyer location." While it can be easy to figure out a general shipping cost for U.S. customers, it's nearly impossible to do so for overseas buyers. Therefore, I would strongly suggest choosing the "Calculated" option.

If you don't want to ship internationally at all, neither through Global Shipping nor on your own, then uncheck the box next to "Sell internationally through the Global Shipping Program" and leave "None" as the option under "Other shipping options."

If you do choose to ship internationally, you can exclude shipping locations if you prefer not to sell to certain countries. If you are using EBay's Global Shipping program, there is no reason to do this as they assume all responsibility for international packages. However, if you are shipping directly to international customers, you may want to exclude problem locations.

Packaging

Finally, you are now at the Package weight & dimensions section, where you will put in the weight of the package. First, eBay has a Package type field where you can choose from four options: "Letter," "Large Envelope," "Package (or thick envelope)," or "Large Package." If you are selling small to mid-size items, you can simply select the Package (or thick envelope) option. That is the only option I have ever chosen.

Next is a field for the box dimensions. The good news is you can altogether skip this! When you go to ship the item, and it is going via Parcel or Priority, you will enter the box dimensions then; however, you never need to add the box size for Media or First Class. And even if you do fill out the box size when printing the label, it doesn't have to be exact; just make sure your box isn't larger than 12x12x12 inches, and you'll be fine.

Last is the field to enter the Weight of the package. If you are shipping something that weighs 16 ounces or less, simply choose the first option, "1 lb. or less," and enter the ounces. Here's a tip: No matter how many ounces the package weighs, put in 16 ounces. Yes, it will result in slightly overcharging some packages; but just chalk up any additional funds to your handling fee.

For items weighing a pound or more, select the range as I talked about earlier, i.e., 1 to 2 pounds, 2 to 3 pounds, 3 to 4 pounds, etc. Note that even if you are offering "free shipping" for domestic customers, you'll still want to enter the weight dimensions for international customers and for US customers who may choose to upgrade their shipping. But again, you just need to select a RANGE, not enter in the exact weight.

And that's all there is to do in the shipping section of your listing!

TIP: Here's a tip that will save you time when listing. Instead of starting from scratch every time you need to create a new listing, open a listing you currently have life and click on the "Sell Similar" option. Then you can just change all of the item specifics, including the shipping options and weight. This makes your listing time fly by as you don't have to set up the shipping section from scratch for every single listing.

PRINTING SHIPPING LABELS ON EBAY

Paying for and printing your labels through eBay is not only fast and easy but much more cost-effective than taking your shipments to the Post Office for postage!

So, you have boxes, packing materials, and a digital scale. You understand the four main USPS shipping categories (Media Mail, First Class Mail, Parcel Select, and Priority Mail). And you know how to set up the Calculated Shipping in your eBay listings quickly. You've sold an item, the buyer has paid, and now it's time to print the shipping label!

When you have an eBay account, printing a label from the comfort of your own home couldn't be any easier! In "My eBay" is your list of "Sold" items. Next to the items that have sold is a drop-down menu where you can find options such as "Contact Buyer" or "Resolve a Problem."

There is also a Send an Invoice option. Note that some buyers WANT you to send them an invoice after they buy an item, even though the shipping options are already set up for them. Fortunately, a quick click sends an invoice, so be prepared to do that occasionally.

Remember that eBay gives buyers four days to pay for their items, so don't hound customers who are slow to pay. If you don't receive payment immediately, you send an invoice. Then the day before payment is due, you send a "friendly" reminder that their payment is due by the following business day. If they don't pay by the next day, open a case using the "Resolve a Problem" option.

Once a customer pays for their item, the default on that drop-down menu is Print Shipping Label. All you need to do is click on that link, and you will be taken to EBay's label printing screen. Please note that you may have to log in again to do this as the system usually wants to confirm you are who you say you are.

The eBay label printing screen has Print your shipping label at the top, along with a summary of the order. Listed will be what the buyer paid for the item and how much they paid for shipping (unless you offered free shipping, in which case that number will be 0). On the left-hand side will be the buyer's address as well as your address.

In the middle of the screen is the section called Select package type. Since you set up your shipping preferences when you created your listing, the United States Postal Service will be the default Carrier. Choose your Package type, Custom size if you are shipping using your own box or regular Priority Mail or Carrier packages if you are using a USPS Flat Rate box or envelope.

For Custom size, simply enter the weight and size of the box. Again, if the package is over one pound, you don't have to enter ounces; if it weighs 1 pound 8 ounces, you can simply enter 2 pounds 0 ounces. If the package is under one pound, you will want to enter in the ounces to get the best

First-Class rate available.

If you are using a USPS Priority Mail FLAT RATE box, select Carrier packages to choose which box or envelope you are using. You do not have to enter weight or dimension if you are shipping in a Flat Rate box or envelope.

Next is the Select section service. Here is where you will choose which shipping service your package will be shipped through, which for most people is USPS. The service the buyer paid for (usually the first option you gave them) will be the default option. However, you can play around with the options to see if you can get a better rate.

Let's say you sold a book that has a shipping weight of 2 pounds. The buyer selected the Media Mail option, which was the first choice given to them. Since you already had 2 pounds as the weight in the listing, there is nothing more for you to do. The Carrier is the United States Postal Service. The Shipping Service is Media Mail. The weight is 2 pounds. Since all the fields are correct, all you need to do is click on the blue "Purchase Postage" icon on the right. You will be directed to your payment method (again, you may need to log in), where you will confirm the purchase of the label. The money to pay for the postage will be taken out of your bank account, and the label will print!

On the other hand, let's say you listed a coffee mug in the 1-2-pound range, and Parcel Select was the default option. Change it to the Priority Mail option to see what the price on the screen changes to. Depending on where the buyer lives, the price could go up or down. Let's say it goes down to a lower rate. That means you can ship the mug in a free Priority Mail box, and the buyer will get it faster than if it were going through Parcel Select, and you will profit a small handling fee from the excess!

However, you may find that Parcel Select IS the best price, so you can just stick with that. When you shop online, you get FREE tracking with First Class, Parcel, and Priority (Media Mail tracking has a small fee). You will also notice a discount on First Class and Priority shipping for printing the labels online. The free tracking and discount postage are two of the best reasons for shipping online!

Before printing the shipping label, you can also add in Protection, such as Require Signature or Added Insurance. You can also decide if you want to Customize your label by displaying the postage cost or adding custom text.

I DO have the Send a message to the buyer field filled out so that the customer gets a confirmation when their item has shipped along with the tracking number.

So, you've chosen your shipping service and double-checked the weight. Everything is ready to go, so now all you have to do is click on the big blue Purchase and print label button. When you print the label, the money for the postage will be taken out of your account and paid directly to the United States Postal Service. eBay and your bank handle the entire transaction for you.

Note that if you offered "free shipping," the postage cost will also be taken out of your account. So, if you sell a shirt for $15, offer free shipping, and it costs $5 to ship, don't be surprised when your balance ends up being under $10 after you pay for postage and eBay fees, which are deducted after each transaction.

After you print your label, you also have the option of printing a packing slip. Simply click on Open packing slip if you would like to print one. I always include a packing slip in my orders, but not all sellers do. Again, the decision is yours to make.

Once your label has been printed, both you and the buyer will receive notice from eBay that the package has shipped. The tracking information will be included in this notice, and it will also be uploaded onto the item transaction page for both you and your buyer to access on your respective My eBay pages. This is a beautiful feature as you, your customer, and eBay now have confirmation from the USPS that the label has been printed. You don't have to type in tracking manually, and if there are any issues with a lost package, you'll be able to show that you indeed did ship the item quickly.

Now that you have your label, all that is left to do is to seal up your package and attach the label to it! Use packing tape to adhere the label to the package. It usually takes me three miniature pieces to cover the label and to make sure it is stuck on tightly. You should also cover the barcode on the shipping label with tape to protect it from the post office sorting machines. It is also essential to cover the address and the return address as well. However, make sure to do it with transparent tape and not brown packaging tape so that the label, address, and barcode are visible to the shipping staff.

Once your label is affixed to your package, it is ready to be shipped out! If you are at home and can arrange for pickup, you'll definitely want to take advantage of the FREE Carrier Pickup service. As long as you have at least one Priority Mail package, your postal carrier will pick up all of your packages for free. You do need to request package pick up the night before, however.

If you aren't able to be home for Carrier Pickup and need to take your packages to the Post Office, note that you will likely have to stand in line and hand them to a clerk. If you end up shipping out a lot of packages and develop a good relationship with the clerks, they may allow you to leave your packages on the counter simply. If you do hand them directly to a clerk, they can scan them and give you a receipt. Usually, skip this since you have the tracking information from eBay loaded onto your account.

10. TIPS FOR CONTINUED SELLING SUCCESS

T his chapter is a simple list of tips and tricks to keep in mind while you're working on your eBay business. There are many small details about eBay, some more anecdotal than fact, but there is still some truth to be found in the experiences of others. Based on our knowledge, the following points are essential to know when trying to navigate your eBay journey.

Selling Internationally

Selling internationally can be a hassle, but it doesn't have to be. For the most straightforward method, you can utilize eBay's Global Shipping Program by simply selecting this in your shipping preferences while you're creating a new listing.

The Global Shipping Program works by having you send a package to a USA fulfillment center after an international customer buys it. From there, the fulfillment center handles everything from customs to getting the product to the customer. eBay will automatically add any customs fees and additional shipping to the customer's order, and you'll simply spend the same amount you'd spend on shipping any other item without ever seeing anything about these added costs.

While the Global Shipping Program does have added fees for buyers, most are willing to pay these because many products are difficult to procure overseas through other methods. This simplified method of selling internationally is excellent if you don't want to add a lot of headaches but want to be able to offer your products internationally.

How to Avoid Problems with Transactions

One of the biggest keys to being successful on eBay is reducing the number of issues customers have with your services. There are a few things you can keep in mind to make this possible.

These include:

Accurate listings that don't hide defects and have images that show exactly what the buyer should expect when they receive the product.

Fair shipping prices and fast shipping, as customers are not happy to pay inflated rates and want their items as soon as possible. Quick shipping is a huge perk when trying to retain positive feedback.

Always offer PayPal. Don't even consider listing anything and not accepting PayPal payments. Not only are most eBay users also using PayPal, but even if they aren't, PayPal can process all other types of payments as well, including credit card and debit cards.

Always provide a tracking number. Not only does this show the item is actually being shipped, but if it should get lost in the post, it makes it much easier to track down and remedy the situation later.

Never ship before a payment post. This should go without saying, but some fraudulent buyers on eBay try to buy items, never pay, and receive them before closing down their accounts and disappearing forever.

What happens when someone doesn't pay?

In the event that someone doesn't pay in a few days following an auction or fixed price listing, there are a few things to keep an eye out for. This includes:

Is the eBay account still active? If it isn't, you should file a case immediately with eBay.

If they are still active eBay users, try contacting them before contacting eBay support. You may be able to guide them through the process if they're new buyers or determine that they have no intention of following through on the order.

Open a case a few days after payment hasn't come through. The absolute latest is 32 days after the end of the auction or fixed price listing.

If they have made a payment but it hasn't been electronically approved, wait an additional week before taking action.

Stock seasonal items

Whenever possible, take advantage of holidays and seasonal trends. Staying abreast of the season can make for a massive increase in sales for a temporary period of time. Take the time to add holiday greetings and seasonal tidbits to your packing slips and email correspondences. Embracing the current holiday is an easy way to draw in more buyers.

Study the Competition

One thing people fail to do when running an eBay business is take the time to understand what their competition is doing with the same types of products. We suggested this before, but it deserves to be repeated. Taking the time to view other listings for the products you are trying to sell is how you can improve on their approach. If you read their listing and notice it doesn't include a detail you think it should, then it's evident that you should include it. Likewise, if they list something you didn't think of and it impresses you, then take a leaf out of their book and do the same thing.

With an eBay store, this becomes especially important. Taking the time to study what has worked for other successful eBay entrepreneurs can teach you far more than shooting the breeze ever will. You don't want to be exactly like the competition, but you want to take the best of what they offer and then fill in the holes of what they don't offer as well to exceed them.

Be friendly

While buyers can be picky, ask too many questions, and are generally mean-spirited or conniving at times, it is essential to remember that old adage, "The customer is always right." This doesn't mean you have to bend over backward to appease a scammer, but it does mean that you should be polite, always address people's issues with measures to resolve the problem and be approachable in general. If someone asks a question, answer it thoroughly and without any snark. Being grumpy may just be your personality, but it doesn't translate well into sales or retaining excellent feedback scores.

Accept returns

It may seem counter-intuitive starting out, as all returns come with a bit of loss in profits, but the truth of the matter is that it's difficult to avoid these anyway. If the buyer has a legitimate reason for a return, then eBay will allow them to open a case against you and force a return anyway. If the buyer doesn't have a legitimate case, they can just as quickly try to open a case, and sometimes they may even win. It's honestly less of a headache just to accept returns as most retail stores would. If you must, you can charge a restocking fee for those returns that aren't due to defects or other issues on your end.

If you take the time to write excellent descriptions, take excellent pictures, and ship your items correctly, returns will be minimized. Make it a policy that you will accept returns for 30 days, but also make it a policy that the buyer must pay return shipping. If there's a defect of some type, you can do the right thing and pay for the return costs yourself anyway.

Write at an 8th-grade level

One problem many educated people have is that they use big words. The truth is that many buyers may not be as educated, and the use of simple language tends to work better for sales, journalism, and just about anything other than poetry and fiction. Writing at an 8th-grade level will be intelligent enough that nobody well educated will feel like you're insulting their intelligence, but it will also be simple enough that anyone without an excellent education won't feel like you're insulting their intelligence. Naturally, if you're selling items in a niche that relies heavily on jargon, you can still include this jargon in your listings.

Research products frequently

Stay on top of the trends! New products are coming out all the time, and your suppliers are likely adding new items to their inventory as well. Try to stay on top of new products as they are released, as a new product on the market is typically going to sell better before other sellers catch on to the sales and drive down the prices. New products are your chance for a boost in sales, and this can be a relatively frequent event if you're genuinely taking the time to handle your product research on a frequent basis.

Continue to shop

Just because you found some great items during your first thrift store or garage sale run doesn't mean that these items are going to sell the way you hoped. They might not even sell at all. The point is that businesses are constantly getting new inventory that they can sell. You, too, need to make sure that you keep stocking up your personal inventory. Inventories and thrift stores are constantly changing, so you may not see identical items twice. Garage sales last a few days. Make time on a weekly basis to go around to your favorite thrift stores and look through the clothing. It might be a tedious task, but if it's a part of your routine, it will get more accessible, and you will begin to find it becomes a habit.

AUCTION STRATEGIES
Don't bother with reserved prices

Auctions with reserved prices are a waste of everyone's time. If you have a set price in mind, just list it as a fixed price and wait for the sale. People bidding on auctions are usually looking for a good deal. While a good bidding war may push it into retail pricing (sometimes above), the general bidder is going to bow out of a silent auction and never be faced with the dilemma of how bad they want to win this item they've been watching and potentially bidding on all week. Reserved auctions do not help you make sales.

List auctions on Sunday afternoons

Sundays tend to be a high-traffic time because a large portion of the population has Sundays off. Auctions that end on Sunday afternoons will often see higher returns simply because the traffic on eBay is more significant. For those on the east coast in the USA, listing between 6-9 PM allows for west coast folk to also get in on the action. The more people that see the listing within the last few hours, the better your chances of selling your auctioned items at a higher price.

Use auctions for rare items

For everyday items, there's really no reason to be using auction-style listings. Auctions are better for items that either don't have an obvious price point or items that are so rare that they only come up once in a blue moon. If you have an item that is rare enough to demand a large sum of money, then take the time to promote this in communities that are likely to seek this item. For example, if you have a phonograph made in the 1940s and it's believed only a few hundred still exist in working order, then you need to scour the internet and social media for groups that collect these types of items and let them know you have it on eBay and point them in the right direction. Maybe start a dialogue as well. They may be able to point you to folks that are willing to sell similar items.

WORK HARD TO BE SUCCESSFUL

While your goal is likely to leave behind a grueling job that doesn't pay well and forces you to be somewhere at a particular time every day, the truth about work is that it takes time and effort. Working hard is the only way you will succeed. Very few people have ever become financially stable by goofing off, and even when they did, there usually comes a time when their lack of initiative puts their business under.

Most eBay businesses get started with little or no money out of pocket. Sellers begin by listing items they already have around the house. As time goes by, they decide eBay is a pretty decent way to make a few extra bucks.

The next step may be to sell a few things for friends and neighbors. Maybe, they check out a yard sale, garage sale, or local estate sale, and then see what is available at local thrift stores.

If these sellers need financing, it typically comes from their credit cards.

Up until now, that has been the extent of financing available to eBay sellers. Banks are not too obliging when they hear the words "eBay" and "business" used together. All too often, negative connotations come to mind, and the banker ends up telling you it is "a great concept, but _____." (You can fill in the blank.)

Kabbage is another financing option available to eBay and Amazon sellers. Kabbage offers small business loans from $500 to $100,000 to online sellers based on sales data from their eBay and Amazon accounts. Their finance rates are not cheap. I paid $90.00 in interest and fees on a $500 loan. The good thing is you get the money quickly. Most often, within an hour or less of applying. It is deposited directly into your linked bank account, and payments are deducted from your account.

If you have a brick-and-mortar location or a connection with a local banker, more options may open to you, but for most sellers—the only choice is to use their credit card or get a short-term loan from Kabbage.

How scary is that?

I am not telling you this to discourage you from running a Kickstarter; instead, I am trying to help you understand how important it is to have a plan and thoroughly research your project before you get started.

The first thing you need to know about Kickstarter is it is not about getting money to fund your business. It is about getting money to support a project.

So, if you need to raise $100,000 so you can start selling iPhones on eBay, it is not going to happen. Not on Kickstarter anyway. If your business makes custom cases for the iPhone 5 and 6 with custom graphics, or a hot new design you created, Kickstarter just might be the ticket to help you launch your business.

The reason custom iPhone cases could get funded is they are a unique project. If your graphics are cool enough, or if the design is unique and stands out head and shoulders over what is available on the market—it just may go viral and grab the interest of backers.

Here is another example.

If you ask for $25,000 to start an online CD store, you are unlikely to attract any backers except your mom and your Uncle Bob (and even they may be a hard sell). If you are the lead singer in a local or regional band, you could run a Kickstarter to raise the cash to press your first CD. That could grab a whole lot of backers, as would a CD of local school kids singing regional folk songs or Christmas carols.

Do you understand the difference?

A Kickstarter is something you use to launch a unique one-time project, not to fund an ongoing business. That is not to say you cannot support a string of similar projects that turn into an entire product line for your eBay store. If you run a successful Kickstarter to fund a CD for a local band, there is nothing to stop you from running another Kickstarter for the same band's next album or an entire series of albums for many local or regional groups.

It is all about breaking your goal down into a series of viable projects.

Avoid eBay listing add-ons

eBay offers a number of add-ons you can apply to your listings. This includes things like templates, bolded auction text, and highlighted auctions in search listings. These things don't do much to help you sell, and they just rack up the cost. Think about it. How often have you bought items that took advantage of these so-called promotional tools? Not very often, I'd assume. About the only time it makes sense is with high-dollar items that are extremely rare and actually stand out on their own anyway.

Leave feedback for your buyer

Once the sale is complete on eBay, make sure that you're returning feedback to the buyer. Buyers like to receive positive feedback just as much as the seller does. Be honest when leaving your feedback. If they were difficult to work with, let other sellers know that. You want to make the buyer know how you felt about the experience as well. Maybe they did not realize that they were challenging. However, before you post this for the public to see, let the buyer know in private.

Ask your former buyers for advice

More than likely, your eBay buyers have purchased clothing from the website in the past. They know what to look for, what to buy, and what they want to see in a seller. Don't be afraid to ask them for advice on your listings or recommend items to them that you think they might like. The buyers will be flattered that you're taking the time to gain their insights into your business.

These are just a few tips that might help you in setting up a successful eBay selling business. Just because you find initial success doesn't mean that there isn't room for improvement. Take time to think of ways to make your items stand out and sell more frequently. Things change, so you need to move with the flow. Change can be good, and knowing what people like to buy is a huge plus to making sure you're making the big bucks by using eBay to sell the clothing you bought at a deep discount yourself!

Try new things

If you find that your methods didn't get you as much money as you hoped to receive, try new things. Once you find your niche, you will be able to sell your items like a pro without much effort. Try taking your pictures in different ways, using different and unique ways to describe your items and different ways to list the items. By gaining ideas from other sellers, you can make your own successful methods for selling your clothing. Another good thing to try is visiting thrift stores and garage sales in different parts of the city. Each demographic area will have different offerings, and they might surprise you.

11. HOW TO MAKE SIX FIGURES ON EBAY

This is the final step in the process of creating a successful eBay business, and it's basically the essential step that will allow you to take your business from something small to something life-changing.

Hopefully, when you have started selling on eBay (if you haven't already), and you get to this point in your eBay business career, you have a set amount of processes already in order, and it's a matter of just doing it (and being creative of course!).

This is where automation comes into play, and it's the stairs that will lead you to the big bucks! Without automation, you will either be slaving away for many, many hours each and every day on your eBay business, whether that be to research items, list them, or ship them, or you will suddenly find that your income is plateauing and you have no idea why.

Automation is going to give you more time to work ON your business rather than IN your business. This is crucial if you want to take your business further. Below are strategies that you can apply to begin automation and then take your skills to the next level.

AUTOMATION TOOLS

Turbo Lister

This is a tool that is highly recommended for small and medium-sized eBay businesses because it will allow you to start automating some of the more basic things, such as listings.

Best of all, it's a tool that can be downloaded directly from eBay for free (just Google it).

Turbo Lister simply lets you work on your listings offline, plugging all your listings into the software while you're offline, bit by bit or all at once and then uploading them together at your discretion when you are online.

Why is it beneficial to me?

It's fantastic because it means you won't be losing any of your listings while you're creating them online (you won't believe how many times I've accidentally clicked "Refresh" or "Back" in my browser while I am creating a listing).

Also, it allows you to create all your listings in one go, at any time in the week, and upload them at a more appropriate time (to maximize auction sales!).

Selling manager

Selling Manager is a tool that you can use to help you sell your items on eBay. It's available online and doesn't require any downloads.

You can Google it and find it (it's affiliated with eBay), and it's free! It is, however, a more limited version of Selling Manager Pro, which requires a paid subscription.

Using this tool, you can have all your product listings and item information in one place, never missing a thing!

Also, it groups all your items together so you can more easily complete bulk tasks, such as listing items, relisting items, leaving feedback, sending messages, invoicing, and printing shipping labels.

Why is it beneficial to me?

Using Selling Manager, you can speed up the amount of time you spend on basic tasks required to sell items, invoice customers, print shipping labels, and leave feedback.

This will give you more time to do other vital things like physically ship the items or even search for new product lines.

Selling manager pro

Selling Manager Pro is pretty much the same as Selling Manager, except it has a few added benefits.

It's also a paid program that requires you to subscribe. It costs approximately $10 a month; however, the actual price depends on your location and which country's eBay you intend to use it on.

Why is it beneficial to me?

This is where the actual benefits of automation come into play.

Firstly, using the Pro version will allow you to print out detailed sales records and evaluations, which can help you to see which products are selling better than others, and at what times and days (so you can maximize auction sales!).

Also, you can monitor accurate inventory details, like keeping a count of how much stock you have left without checking in your garage or shed.

The benefit of using Selling Manager Pro – is you can automate those mundane tasks such as emailing customers after they purchase items, pay for items, or items are marked as shipped. You can automate feedback and even automate relisting schedules and relisting of unsold items.

Like I said above, this is where the actual benefits of automation come into play because you suddenly start to see massive decreases in the amount of time you spend online, and when you are online, you're just managing your business because everything, especially the mundane tasks, is automatically done for you.

Shipworks

This is a tool that is awesome for US eBay sellers (unfortunately, due to the specific programming required for each shipping provider, it's only available in the US as of the time of writing this eBook).

It's a tool that will automatically take the shipping addresses of your completed listings and import the recipient information into your shipping carrier's online shipping forms. It's linked to many US carriers, such as FedEx and UPS, plus a few more!

Why is it beneficial to me?

This will save you so much time writing out or even printing shipping labels, making things much easier when it comes to the shipping part of your business.

Other automated listing software

Here are some more programs and online tools you can use. I have not discussed them individually because I only really have ever used both Turbo Lister and Selling Manager Pro myself. I have messed around with Auctiva before, but not for too long.

Here is the list:

- http://www.auctiva.com

- http://www.auctionwizard.com

- http://www.marketblast.com

- http://www.vendio.com

Automation: in a completely new light!

This idea I'm about to write about might seem quite ridiculous on how much your business is making, but it's something you need to consider when you start getting more prominent (which may only be once you move to your own website – more on this below!).

I'm talking about hiring someone to work in your business for you.

Hire some young students to help you out with the shipping side of things because you don't have the time, nor do you want to print out shipping labels, pack items, and go to the post office every day.

Combining this with the automation tools you used for listing new products, I had most of my business automated and found that the only time I spent online was working on researching new products and markets.

If that's something you can't do, maybe consider someone in your family? A brother? Sister? Mother? Grandparent?

Is there anyone around you that can help you out for an hour or so a day with your business?

When hiring someone "in real life," it's usually for your physical work, such as shipping.

The reason I say "in real life" is that you can actually hire a virtual assistant to help you out with the virtual work, such as listings, feedback, etc., especially if you don't want to invest in an automation tool.

I recommend checking out "Upkork" to find people you can hire.

Simply post up a job with the work you're offering, such as "eBay listing creation," and test out a few workers with some small jobs.

Hire them for a month to test them out. If there are no issues, keep them longer!

Definitely check out both those sites, and even read up on some tutorials on how they work so you can learn more about it. Unfortunately, I can't go into much detail about it here because I can ramble on about it so much that it would fit into another eBook of its own.

USING A THIRD-PARTY SHIPPING PROVIDER

EBay's shipping label service is excellent, but sometimes you need a little more oomph to boost your sales and simplify things even more.

Try to use Stamps.com. It's a great alternative. Other people have had good luck using Endicia to handle their shipping needs. Both services charge a monthly service fee for using them.

I know what you're thinking. Wait a minute; I'm trying to save money, not spend even more.

Believe me, I understand. The thing you can save a lot of money using Stamps.com to power your eBay shipping. Here's why they use it and how it saves money.

What got eBay sellers hooked on Stamps.com is it's the only way they can ship the items first class international without going to the post office and having them print labels for them. If you use eBay's shipping solution or Click-N-Ship, you can only ship internationally using priority or express mail. When doing so, international sales go down because of the extra shipping costs involved. The extra sales you get by offering the less expensive shipping solution more than cover the $15.99 monthly fee.

One of the other reasons people like using Stamps.com is it collects information from all of the platforms you sell on and lets them handle all of your shipping from one central location. For people, that means they can ship the items to sell on eBay, Amazon, bid Start, and your own website, all from the same program console.

I don't have to jump from site to site to ship everything. If I need to look up shipping info for an item—it's all on Stamps.com.

It's convenient. I like that. It's worth the extra fifteen dollars a month it costs me to use the service.

To get started with Stamps.com, just visit the following link http://www.stamps.com/. Select get started to register for a new account. Most times, they offer a sign-up special that gives you a free postal scale, $25.00 in free shipping credits, and miscellaneous other goodies, along with a one-month free trial.

Once you're ready to go, you can connect all your seller accounts.

What I'm going to do next is give you a quick walkthrough on how to connect your merchant accounts and how to print postage using Stamps.com. (I assume Endicia works similar to this, but I've never used that service, so I can't provide you with specifics.)

Don't worry. I'll make this quick and painless.

Setup shipping accounts

There are two ways to set up your accounts. Select Manage Sources in the toolbar at the top of the screen, or select batch from the toolbar in the left-hand column.

Choose Create Profile, and select the data source you want to create.

Printing postage

When you open your Stamp.com dashboard, there is a command bar running across the top of the screen. There are four primary tabs that you'll use over and over again: import orders, manage sources, print, and add orders.

"Import orders" lets you collect your orders from all of the sites you sell on and bring them into Stamps.com.

Manages sources and allows you to add, delete, or edit data streams.

Add order allows you to print a label for a package where the customer is not included in any of your data streams. An example is when I send out a review copy of one of my books. The recipient is not in my data stream, so I need to set up a one-time shipment.

Print pulls up the screen to print your shipping label

Okay, let's assume you just sat down at your desk, and you're ready to start shipping. What do you do?

Select <import orders> from the top menu bar; you'll be prompted several times about actions that are in progress. Most often, Stamps.com wants permission to update addresses to match the official address in the postal system computer. Click okay.

After a little while, all your orders will appear in a spreadsheet in the middle of the screen. Select the item you want to mail, and click on the recipient name—the shipping screen for that customer.

Off to the left-hand side of the screen, you will see your name and address. Below that, you will find your client's name and address. You can make whatever changes you need to the shipping address here. The following line is labeled email address. Check the box in front of it, and it will populate with your customer's email address. When you check this, it will send shipping and tracking info to your buyer. The box right after this is the cost code. You can make an internal note here if you are tracking categories for shipping.

The next column contains your shipping options.

If you have a USB scale, it will transfer the weight with the click of a button. I usually round up to the next ounce or two, depending on the item I'm shipping. That gives me a little wiggle room for the label and tape.

After this, you need to choose the type of mailpiece—package, thick envelope, etc.

Then you select the mail class:

- First Class
- Priority Mail
- Express Mail
- Parcel Post
- Media Mail

Place a checkmark on the tab to select the mail class. When you do this, it will show the cost of that service. Some classes get blanked out if you can't choose them to ship that particular item. As an example, packages over thirteen ounces cannot be sent by first-class, so the shipping method would not be available for you to select.

After this, you choose tracking options—delivery confirmation (free with most shipping methods), signature confirmation (an additional $2.35), or none (tracking is not available on flats sent by first class).

Just below this, there is a line labeled options where you can add—certified, USPS insurance, registered, or COD delivery.

The next option lets you select insurance. You can select none or Stamps.com. Your final choice is whether you want to hide the postage cost so buyers cannot see it. If you marked your shipping up a lot, make sure you choose this option.

After you've selected all of your options, click <save> at the bottom of the box. When you do this, a green circle should appear in front of the <order id> on the spreadsheet. To print your postage, choose <print> from the menu bar at the top of the screen. You should see a pop-up that shows the printer's name and details. Select <print> at the bottom of the screen to print your label.

International shipping with stamps.com

Setting up an order for international delivery is very similar to shipping a domestic order. The only difference is you need to complete a customs form.

Here is what you need to do to fill out the online customs form.

Click on the customs form, and it will display a pop-up box for you to fill out. At the top of the form, it asks for a phone number. If your customer lists a number with eBay, it will prepopulate. If they didn't give me their number, I just filled in 999-999-9999. Otherwise, it will not let you continue.

Where it asks for content, you have several options. Choose <merchandise>. In the box next to this type is a short description. I usually type articles or print them.

About midway down the page, there is a section labeled itemized package contents. The first box asks for the quantity or number of items you are shipping. After that, it asks for a short description of what you are shipping. It should prepopulate from your eBay item description. If the description is too long, you need to shorten it, or the form will not process correctly. The next thing it asks you for is the weight of just the item (without the packaging).

When you've completed all the items, the box at the end of this line asks to add an item. Check that box, and it will move your description into the box below that line.

At the bottom of the pop-up box is a form you need to check. It begins with "I acknowledge...." Once you select the check box, the pop-up box disappears, and you can print your item like normal.

TAX INFORMATION FOR SELLERS ON EBAY

As a seller on eBay, you are obligated to follow all the applicable tax laws according to eBay's tax policy. Selling to buyers in specific states like the US, Australia, New Zealand, United Kingdom, or the European Union requires you to pay a specific type of taxes on your sales. These include Goods and Services Tax and/or Value Added Tax (VAT).

What are your tax responsibilities as a seller?

As a seller, you are responsible for paying all eBay fees and taxes applied to your sales by eBay according to your location as per the rules of eBay's tax policy. Your tax responsibilities as a seller include:

- Payment of sales tax on your eBay sales.
- Payment of income tax on your eBay sales.
- Inform your overseas buyers about the payment of import charges.
- Validation of tax collection on sales transactions.

Income Tax

If you are a seller on eBay, then the Law requires you to declare your income and pay corresponding taxes on income earned through eBay sales. Irrespective of whether you are selling as a hobby or as a full-fledged business, you have to report your eBay income at a certain level of earning. When your gross eBay sales reach $20000 or when you have completed 200 transactions in one calendar year, then you have to report your earnings from eBay sales to the IRS and start paying income tax on it.

Internet Sales Tax in the U.S.

Sales tax is the ultimate pandora's box in the face of e-commerce sellers. Obtaining sales tax on e-commerce sales is one of the most significant ways for countries to meet their budget shortfalls since the COVID-19 pandemic has boosted online sales by more than 30%.

Depending on the US state you are based in, you may be required to collect internet sales tax on your eBay sales and transactions. As of now, 46 states and jurisdictions in the US require sellers to collect internet sales tax. However, one important thing to know is that eBay collects sales tax from buyers on the seller's behalf.

eBay collects internet sales tax by including the amount of sales tax within the order receipt sent to the buyer before order processing. After payment, this tax is automatically deducted and sent for remittance to the applicable taxing authority of the particular jurisdiction.

You must know that internet sales tax is paid by the buyer, and eBay will collect it on your behalf. The calculation, collection, and remittance of sales tax is eBay's responsibility, so you don't have to take any action in this regard.

However, sellers are responsible for charging sales tax only in states where they are authorized to do so. For this purpose, you need to acquire a license or permit from each state where you are required to charge sales tax, and you must provide eBay with the sales tax collection permit. You should specify each state where you are required to charge sales tax by setting up the tax table facility of eBay.

Here's how you can set up a tax table on eBay:

1. Go to the sales tax table page on eBay's website.
2. Fill in the table with the tax rates for states where you are required to charge sales tax.
3. Select the "Also charge sales tax on S&H" tab if you are required by the state to charge tax on shipping and handling as well.
4. Select "Save."

After completing the setup process for a tax table, you are required to specify in your listings that you are charging sales tax on a particular item. Here's how you can do that:

1. Open the listing form and select the table saying "Charge sales tax according to the sales tax table."

2. If you want to make changes to the tax table, then open it by selecting "View sales tax table."

3. Complete the listing form and select "Preview listing" or "Save and continue later."

It is essential to know that any changes you make in your tax table will not be automatically updated in your live or currently active listings. For this, you need to revise any active listings so that the changes in your tax table are applied to them. For listings that you create after changing your tax table, the information will already appear updated.

Tax for buyers outside the U.S.

Internet sales tax is termed as Value Added Tax (VAT) in the UK and EU, while in Australia (AU)and New Zealand (NZ), it is known as Good & Services Tax (GST).

VAT in UK and EU

VAT is the tax applied on consumer spending and is essentially the same concept as sales tax in the U.S. Unlike income tax, VAT is not required to be paid by the seller but rather to be paid by the buyer and is added to the item cost while buying. If you intend to sell your goods in the UK or EU, then you are required to register yourself for VAT collection. You can register for VAT collection and return filings online on the website of the local tax authority.

After VAT registration, you will receive a VAT identification which you are required to display next to your listings on the eBay website by updating your seller information.

VAT registration becomes compulsory in the UK and EU in the following three situations:

1. Sale of goods beyond a threshold defined by local authorities.
2. If you are selling goods through a non-resident seller from a local warehouse.
3. In the case of the EU only, sales across borders beyond the specified distance sales thresholds. On the basis of the country where goods are delivered, currently, the distance sales thresholds are set to either EUR 35,000 or EUR 100,000.

Sellers are required to make a VAT registration in each EU state where their sales exceed EUR 10,000 or £8,818. The VAT rates in the EU are different for different countries and depend on the type of items sold.

Since the exit of the UK from the EU, the VAT requirements have been different in the UK. Currently, the UK has set a VAT rate of 20%, but there is an exception of 5% and 0% for certain items as well. This information can be obtained from the website of the UK government, i.e., gov.uk.

GST in AU and NZ

Sales tax in the US is called GST in AU and NZ. eBay is required to collect GST from buyers from AU and NZ who make an order up to AU $1000 and

NZ $1000. eBay automatically adds this tax to the order total while checking out and deducts it from the buyer's payment, and sends it for remittance to the Australian Taxation Office (ATO) or NZ Inland Revenue Department (IRD). For orders exceeding a value of $1000, the GST is collected at the borders of Australia and New Zealand and not by eBay.

Sellers are required to include all tax details of eBay and their custom code for AU and NZ on the package before shipping. These include:

- Australia: eBay's ABN #64 652 016 681 Code: PAID
- New Zealand: eBay's IRD #126-101-678 Code: PAID

Other countries

eBay charges sales tax, VAT, or GST from buyers in other countries depending upon the particular legislation and policies of that country. This is done by any means available to eBay, and the tax remittance is done to the local tax authority of that country. If tax needs to be collected from an overseas buyer, eBay will add the tax information and the delivery address of the buyer, which the seller is required to add to the parcel before shipping.

Informing overseas buyers about import charges

Certain import charges are applied to items when you sell to buyers outside of the US. These import charges include taxes and customs duties. The rate of these charges is determined by the country where the item is being shipped and is usually dependent upon the country of origin, parcel weight, and dimensions.

For some countries, import charges are collected by eBay while the buyer pays for their order. For orders where import charges are not collected by eBay, buyers need to pay additional import charges on receiving their parcel or while clearing their parcel through custom checking.

Sellers, including international shipping, cannot include these import charges in the cost of the item or shipping charges. You must inform your buyer about this in your listing.

CONCLUSION

There is no ultimate truth or divine revelation on how to become a successful eBay seller. Only those who are passionate and have a fundamental business mindset can shine on eBay. You should be realistic and very practical about your business ideas. You have to ensure that you will get the best price and that the supply of your products will be secured all the time. Every now and then, you have to switch your interest according to the market demand to stay competitive. Don't stop researching and keep enough profit margins to feed your business and expand it if needed. Try to compete with other sellers through your customer service, price, and branding skills. Always follow eBay's rules and regulations and do not attempt to violate any of those. Try to learn from other sellers. Watch what they are doing and do it better than them. Learn from successful sellers and collect tips from them. Try to explore new features and possibilities on eBay every now and then. No one will guarantee you a 100% success rate, and only YOU can make it happen with confidence and effort. Never stop striving for more; Never stop selling more.

Now that you have a better idea of how to make money selling on eBay, the question is: Does it grab you. If so, I encourage you to check it out further and see what you can sell on eBay.

If you really want eBay success, you need to implement everything I am teaching you and do it properly, with persistence!

Running an eBay business is not a get-rich-quick scheme; it's something that you need to build from scratch and nourish with determination. Only then will you begin to see long-lasting results.

Finally, just remember it's possible, and once you get the ball rolling, you'll see it's actually not as complex as it might seem!

How'd You Enjoyed Reading *How to Sell on eBay for Beginners*?

I want to say thank you for purchasing and reading this book! I hope you enjoyed it and it's provided value to your life. If you enjoyed reading this book and found some benefit in it, I'd love your support and hope that you could take a moment to post a review on Amazon. I'd love to hear from you, even if you have feedback, as it'll help me in ensuring that I improve this book and others in the future.

I want to let you know that your review is critical to me and will help this book reach and impact more people's lives. Thanks for your time and support!

EXTRA: MORE ABOUT SHIPPING METHODS

n the section following, I will give you the best methods and go into more detail when items are on eBay. As a disclaimer, I want to mention that the rates and methods of shipment I talk about below are subject to change by the United States Postal Service, and policies and methods may be different depending upon when you are reading this book. In addition, especially when it comes to the legal flat rate envelopes, many post offices are not accepting items to be shipped if the packages are overly stuffed. This is also true when it comes to the flat rate boxes provided by the USPS. Please be sure to read the fine print at the time of shipping when using any of the methods to assure you are obeying the USPS rules of conduct. I will provide different types of shipping methods, reasons for why you should or shouldn't use the method, the price to ship, and a few other bits of information I feel you may find helpful.

Legal flat rate envelope

Price to Ship: $4.99 online

Size: 9.5x15 inches

Pros of Using This Method: Flat rate cost anywhere in the country regardless of weight, fast shipping, cheapest method possible to ship

Cons of Using This Method: It May be hard to fit item inside, decreased protection with envelope

Be Aware: Some post offices frown on people using the legal flat rate envelopes to ship items other than documents. Be careful when overstuffing and overdoing it with tape.

Where to Purchase: Free on the USPS website

Bubble mailer flat rate

Price to Ship: $5.35 online

Size: 9.5x 12.5 inches

Pros of Using This Method: Added protection over the legal flat rate envelope, flat-rate cost anywhere in the country regardless of weight, very cheap to ship, fast shipping with priority

Cons of Using This Method: Will only be able to fit a petite blazer or sports coat

Be Aware: You may have difficulty fitting items inside. By jamming the item inside too much, you are risking having the item damaged during shipment.

Where to Purchase: Free on the USPS website

Medium flat rate box (2 choices)

Box # 1

Price to Ship: $10.65 online

Size: 11 x 8.5 x 5.5 inches

Pros of Using This Method: Flat rate cost anywhere in the country regardless of weight, can fit most items for less than $11.00, the box protects items very well, fast shipping with priority

Cons of Using This Method: Flat rate postage can be more expensive than other methods if you are shipping to a nearby state

Be Aware: The box must not be overly stuffed or bulging out. The post office will give you a hard time if the content does not fit nicely inside.

Where to Purchase: Free on the USPS website

Box # 2

Price to Ship: $10.65 online

Size: 11-7/8x 3-3/8 x 13-5/8inches

Pros of Using This Method: Flat rate cost anywhere in the country regardless of weight, can fit nearly any item for less than $11.00, the box protects items very well, fast shipping with priority

Cons of Using This Method: Flat rate postage can be more expensive than other methods if you are shipping to a nearby state, medium flat rate box #2 can be more challenging to fit thicker items

Be Aware: The box must not be overly stuffed or bulging out. The post office will give you a hard time if the content does not fit nicely inside.

Where to Purchase: Free on the USPS website

Large flat rate box

Price to Ship: $14.80 online
Size: 12 x 12 x 5.5 inches

Pros of Using This Method: Flat rate cost anywhere in the country regardless of weight, can fit most items for less than $15.00, the box protects items very well, fast shipping with priority

Cons of Using This Method: Cost to ship using this method may eat a lot of your profit; a cheaper alternative is usually available

Be Aware: The box must not be overly stuffed or bulging out. The post office will give you a hard time if the content does not fit nicely inside.

Where to Purchase: Free on the USPS website

Plain box (priority)

Price to Ship: Depends on location and weight
Size: Any size. Beware of huge boxes, as you can be hit with an oversize fee. Also, larger boxes weigh more and will make shipment more expensive.

Weight Limit: None

Pros of Using This Method: Can use any size box (keeping in mind oversize fees), can purchase extra-strong boxes for added protection

Cons of Using This Method: It can be more expensive than using flat rate boxes. You may have to pay for boxes if you cannot get them for free

Be Aware: The price will vary according to weight and location.

Where to Purchase: You can quickly get boxes for free if you ask stores, U-Line, Wal-Mart

Standard post (formerly parcel post)

Price to Ship: Depends on the weight and location

Size: You can use any size box you like

Pros of Using This Method: It can be a cheaper alternative for shipping hefty items (for example, if shipping a lot of five suits across the country)

Cons of Using This Method: Very slow shipping, a better chance of items getting damaged due to increased transit time, can be more expensive than priority depending on location

Be Aware: Very slow shipping. You need to use a plain box; you cannot ship parcels using a priority box. Go above and beyond to protect your items very well when shipping this method.

Where to Purchase: You can quickly get boxes for free if you ask stores, Wal-Mart, U-Line

Regional rate boxes(4 Recommended Choices)

Regional Box A1

Price to Ship: Depends on location

Size: 10 x 7 x 4.75 inches

Weight Limit: 15 pounds

Pros of Using This Method: Ships at a 2-pound rate and can save you money depending on weight and location of shipment, priority mail is speedy shipping, and the box offers excellent protection for items.

Cons of Using This Method: It may be cheaper to ship in a flat rate envelope if the item fits into one.

Be Aware: Price differs by location. There is a weight limit. You must print postage online.

Where to Purchase: Free on the USPS website

Regional Box A2

Price to Ship: Depends on location

Size: 10-15/16 x 2-3/8 x 12-13/16 inches

Weight Limit: 15 pounds

Pros of Using This Method: Ships at a 2-pound rate and can save you money depending on weight and location of shipment, priority mail is swift shipping, and the box offers excellent protection for the item

Cons of Using This Method: It may be cheaper to ship in a flat rate envelope if an item fits into one.

Be Aware: Price differs by location. There is a weight limit. You must print postage online.

Where to Purchase: Free on the USPS website

Regional Box B1

Price to Ship: Depends on location

Size: 12 x 10.25 x 5 inches

Weight Limit: 20 pounds

Pros of Using This Method: Ships at a 4-pound rate and can save you money depending on weight and location of shipment, priority mail is speedy shipping, and the box offers excellent protection for items.

Cons of Using This Method: More expensive than Regional "A" boxes.

Be Aware: Price differs by location. There is a weight limit. You must print postage online.

Where to Purchase: Free on the USPS website

Regional Box B2

Price to Ship: Depends on location

Size: 14-3/8 x 2-7/8 x 15-7/8 inches

Weight Limit: 20 pounds

Pros of Using This Method: Ships at a 4-pound rate and can save you money depending on weight and location of shipment, priority mail is speedy shipping, and the box offers excellent protection for the item.

Cons of Using This Method: More expensive than Regional A boxes

Be Aware: Price differs by location. There is a weight limit. You must print postage online.

Where to Purchase: Free on the USPS website

INTERNATIONAL SHIPPING

When it comes to shipping your items internationally, most of the same rules apply as if you were shipping domestically, but there are a few things you will want to be aware of.

One of the main things you will want to know about shipping internationally is that anything less than 4 pounds is eligible to be shipped via first-class international mail. This differs from domestic shipping, in which you can only ship first-class mail if the item weighs 13 ounces or less. When shipping domestically, first-class mail will not be an option because all blazers, sports coats, and suits will weigh more than 13 ounces.

First-class international mail does have its drawbacks. Some of the issues you may be concerned about are slow shipping times and the lack of tracking. I have found that when shipping first class mail international, the chances of running into a problem—such as buyers claiming they did not receive their items—is significantly increased in comparison to shipping priority international. As a side note, when shipping first class mail, or even priority, perform due diligence when deciding to ship to certain countries. As an example, I have found to have many problems shipping internationally to countries such as Brazil, Russia, and Italy. Ship with caution!

How to ship first class mail international

When shipping first-class international, you will have two main options. It's best to use either a large poly bag or a plain cardboard box. You have to keep in mind the weight limit, so make sure the item and materials weigh less than 4 pounds!

Option #1 Poly Bag

Price to Ship: Depends on location and weight

Size: I like to use 12x15inches or bigger

Weight Limit: Less than 4 pounds

Pros of Using This Method: Poly bag is very lightweight. Using poly bags to ship first class mail versus priority will save you money

Cons of Using This Method: Less protection using a poly bag versus a box. First-class mail is slower, with no tracking included.

Be Aware: Shipments may take months to arrive at the destination. You may want to purchase insurance from a company. Only certain countries are eligible for insurance internationally. I want you to know that if a package does not arrive at a destination, eBay and your bank will likely side with the buyer, and you will lose your money 99 percent of the time. With that in mind, definitely protect yourself by ordering insurance!

Where to Purchase: eBay or Amazon

Option #2 Plain Box

Price to Ship: Depends on location and weight

Size: Any size. Beware of super large boxes, as you can be hit with an oversize fee. Larger boxes weigh more, and you need to keep weight under 4 pounds to ship first class international.
Weight Limit: Less than 4 pounds

Pros of Using This Method: More protection versus poly bag

Cons of Using This Method: Using the box will be heavier, and it may be difficult to keep overall weight under 4 pounds

Be Aware: Shipments may take months to arrive at the destination. You may want to purchase insurance from a company. I use Ship Saver through eBay to insure packages. Only certain countries are eligible for insurance internationally.

Where to Purchase: Get free from stores, U-Line, Wal-Mart

How to ship priority mail international

When shipping priority mail international, you can use all the methods I outlined for shipping domestically, except for the Regional Rate boxes. When using the flat rate boxes internationally, the costs can add up rather quickly.

Legal Flat Rate Envelope
Price to Ship: Depends on location
Size: 9.5x15 inches

Pros of Using This Method: Flat rate cost can save you a lot of money

Cons of Using This Method: It May be hard to fit item inside, decreased protection with envelope

Be Aware: Some post offices frown on people using the legal flat rate envelopes to ship items other than documents. Be careful when overstuffing and overdoing it with tape.

Where to Purchase: Free on the USPS website

Plain Box (Priority Mail International)

Price to Ship: Depends on location and weight

Size: Any size. Beware of super large boxes, as you can be hit with an oversize fee. Also, larger boxes weigh more and will make shipment more expensive.

Weight Limit: None

Pros of Using This Method: Can use any size box (keeping in mind oversize fees), can purchase extra-strong boxes for added protection

Cons of Using This Method: It can become quite expensive based on weight (try to use first-class mail if you can, or use a legal flat rate envelope if the item will fit)

Be Aware: The price will vary according to weight and location.

Where to Purchase: Get free from stores, U-Line, Wal-Mart

Putting It All Together

Hopefully, after reading through this chapter, you have learned how to ship your products on eBay effectively

If you are new to shipping, I can guarantee you will feel overwhelmed. But don't worry; it is normal and expected. Be sure to take your time when first beginning to ship your items, and please use this chapter as a reference to get you moving in the right direction. Before you know it, you will be moving much quicker and will be confident in your shipping abilities.

Honestly, now that you know what methods you can use to ship your products, it's all a matter of figuring out which method will be the cheapest and most effective for each individual item you ship. There are a lot of factors that can play a role when it comes to deciding how to ship an item, so do not rush your decision-making. I congratulate you on getting through this chapter; you have now put yourself in a position to save tons of money throughout the future by learning how to ship like a pro!

Made in the USA
Las Vegas, NV
13 July 2023

74604472R00079